# Mastering Internal
# Processes and
# Procedures

## Book 8

*8 Books to 8 Figures Series*

## Jason Miller

ISBN: 978-1-957217-60-4 (hardcover)
ISBN: 978-1-957217-61-1 (paperback)
ISBN: 978-1-957217-62-8 (ebook)

# TABLE OF CONTENTS

Introduction . . . . . . . . . . . . . . . . . . . . . . . . . . . . . . . v

Chapter 1:  Understanding Internal Processes. . . . . . . . . . 1

Chapter 2:  Analyzing Current Processes . . . . . . . . . . . . 12

Chapter 3:  Designing Effective Processes. . . . . . . . . . . . 29

Chapter 4:  Implementing New Procedures . . . . . . . . . . 40

Chapter 5:  Monitoring and Evaluating Processes. . . . . . 49

Chapter 6:  Technology and Automation . . . . . . . . . . . 58

Chapter 7:  Building a Culture of Process Excellence . . . 73

Conclusion . . . . . . . . . . . . . . . . . . . . . . . . . . . . . . . 87

# INTRODUCTION

Internal processes are the backbone of any successful business. They refer to the activities and tasks within an organization to produce a product or deliver a service. Unlike external processes, which involve interactions with customers or other businesses, internal processes are all about what happens behind the scenes. Examples of internal processes include human resources (HR), production, and logistics. HR handles hiring, training, and employee management. Production is where the actual creation of goods or services takes place. Logistics ensures that everything gets where it needs to be, whether it's materials coming in or finished products going out.

Understanding and optimizing internal processes is crucial for the smooth functioning of any organization. They provide structure and ensure everyone knows their role and how they contribute to the company's goals. Internal processes help keep everything organized and running smoothly, which is essential for achieving business objectives. Without well-defined processes, an organization can quickly become chaotic, leading to missed deadlines, increased costs, and unhappy customers.

Internal processes play a key role in maintaining the efficiency and productivity of a business. Streamlining operations can lead to faster turnaround times, which means that tasks are completed more quickly and customers get their products or services sooner. When operations are streamlined, there is less redundancy and waste, making the business more efficient. For instance, a company that improved its internal processes might eliminate unnecessary steps in its production line, leading to faster and more efficient production.

Boosting productivity is another significant benefit of refining internal processes. When resources and personnel are used optimally, the business can produce more with the same or even fewer inputs. Automation of routine tasks is a common way to enhance productivity. Automating repetitive tasks allows employees to focus on more strategic activities that require human insight and creativity. For example, a company that automated its inventory management system saw a significant increase in productivity, as employees no longer had to spend hours tracking stock levels manually.

To illustrate the impact of internal processes, let's consider a company that significantly improved its efficiency through better internal processes. This company had a production process that was slow and prone to errors. By analyzing and refining their internal processes, they identified bottlenecks and implemented solutions that sped up production and reduced errors. As a result, they saw a substantial improvement in their overall efficiency.

Another example is a company that saw a productivity boost from refining its internal processes. This company had been struggling with managing its growing workforce and the increasing volume of tasks. By implementing an automated HR system, they were able to streamline employee management and free up time for their HR team to focus on strategic initiatives. This led to a noticeable increase in productivity and allowed the company to grow more effectively.

Internal processes are essential for the efficient and productive operation of a business. They provide structure, streamline operations, and boost productivity. By understanding and optimizing these processes, businesses can achieve their goals more effectively and ensure long-term success.

# 1

# UNDERSTANDING INTERNAL PROCESSES

Internal processes are the systematic series of actions we take to accomplish tasks and achieve our goals. From the moment we receive an order to the final delivery of a product or service, internal processes guide each step, ensuring everything runs smoothly and efficiently. Without these processes, our operations would be chaotic and inconsistent, making maintaining quality and meeting customer expectations difficult.

This chapter will explore the importance of internal processes in business operations. We will cover what internal processes are, why they are essential for the overall functioning of an organization, and the different types of processes that exist. By understanding these elements, we can appreciate how well-defined processes contribute to our success and look at ways to optimize them for even better performance.

Internal processes are the procedures and protocols we follow to complete work. They can range from simple tasks, like answering customer inquiries, to more complex activities, such as product development or strategic planning. The key is that they provide a clear framework for how things should be done, which helps ensure consistency and efficiency across the board.

The importance of internal processes cannot be overstated. They play a crucial role in every aspect of our operations. For instance, in production, a standardized process ensures that each product is made to the same standard, minimizing defects and waste. In customer service, clear procedures help our team handle inquiries quickly and effectively, leading to higher customer satisfaction. In management, well-defined processes for decision-making and performance evaluation help us stay aligned with our strategic goals and make informed decisions.

Without internal processes, it would be challenging to achieve any level of efficiency or consistency. Every task would be approached differently, leading to variability in outcomes and a lack of control over the final product or service. This inconsistency can damage our reputation, frustrate employees, and drive customers away. By having structured processes in place, we create a stable environment where everyone knows what is expected and how to achieve it.

## TYPES OF INTERNAL PROCESSES

Internal processes can be broadly categorized into three types: operational, management, and support processes. Each type plays a crucial role in ensuring the smooth functioning of the business.

Operational processes are the core activities that directly contribute to delivering value to our customers. These are the day-to-day tasks that keep the business running. In production, operational processes involve everything from sourcing raw materials to manufacturing products and ensuring they meet quality standards. In marketing, they encompass our strategies and tactics to promote our products or services, such as advertising campaigns and social media outreach. In sales, operational processes include prospecting, engaging with potential customers, closing deals, and providing after-sales support. These processes are vital because they are directly linked to customer satisfaction and revenue generation. By refining these processes, we can enhance the value we provide to our customers, ensuring they receive high-quality products and services promptly.

Management processes, on the other hand, focus on guiding and controlling the organization. These processes include strategic planning, decision-making, and performance management. Strategic planning involves setting long-term goals and determining the best strategies to achieve them. Decision-making processes help us evaluate options and choose the best course of action, whether it's launching a new product or entering a new market. Performance management involves monitoring and evaluating employee performance to ensure that everyone is working toward the organization's goals. These management processes are essential for aligning the efforts of different departments and ensuring that the organization moves in the right direction. They provide the framework for making informed decisions and implementing strategies that drive growth and success.

Support processes are the backbone that provides the necessary resources and support to both operational and management processes. These include human resources, IT support, and accounting. Human resources manage everything related to our workforce, from recruitment and training to employee relations and benefits administration. IT support ensures that our technology infrastructure runs smoothly, providing the tools and systems needed for efficient operations. Accounting handles financial transactions, budgeting, and financial reporting, ensuring that we have a clear picture of our financial health. Support processes might not directly generate revenue, but they are crucial for maintaining the infrastructure that allows operational and management processes to function effectively. They ensure that we have the right people, technology, and financial oversight to achieve our business goals.

Operational processes deliver value to customers, management processes guide and control the organization, and support processes provide the necessary resources and support. Each type of process is integral to the success of the business, and understanding their roles helps us optimize our operations and achieve our objectives. By refining and improving these processes, we can create a more efficient, effective, and resilient organization capable of thriving in a competitive market.

## THE ROLE OF PROCEDURES IN INTERNAL PROCESSES

The role of procedures in internal processes is fundamental to the smooth and efficient operation of any business. Procedures provide a clear roadmap for completing tasks and achieving goals, ensuring that everyone in the organization is on the same page.

Standard Operating Procedures, or SOPs, are detailed, written instructions that describe how to perform specific tasks. SOPs are essential because they ensure consistency and efficiency across the board. When everyone follows the same procedures, the quality of work remains high and predictable. For example, in a manufacturing setting, an SOP might detail the exact steps for operating a piece of machinery, ensuring that each product is made to the same high standard. In a customer service department, an SOP could outline the proper way to handle customer inquiries, ensuring that all customers receive the same level of service.

The importance of SOPs extends to all areas of a business. In marketing, an SOP might describe the process for creating and approving marketing materials, ensuring that all content aligns with the company's brand and messaging. In sales, an SOP could outline the steps for following up with leads, helping to maintain consistency in the sales process and improve conversion rates. These procedures help employees know exactly what is expected of them and provide a clear framework for completing their tasks efficiently.

## THE IMPORTANCE OF DOCUMENTATION

Documentation of procedures is another critical aspect of internal processes. Thorough documentation is crucial for several reasons. First, it provides clarity. When procedures are well-documented, employees can easily understand how to perform their tasks without needing constant supervision or assistance. This clarity reduces confusion and helps employees feel more confident in their roles.

Second, documentation ensures consistency. With written procedures, tasks are completed the same way every time, which is essential for maintaining quality and reliability. This consistency is particularly important in industries where precision and accuracy are critical, such as healthcare or manufacturing.

Third, documentation is vital for training. New employees can quickly get up to speed by referring to documented procedures, reducing the time and resources needed for training. This not only helps new hires become productive more quickly but also ensures they are following the correct procedures from day one.

Finally, thorough documentation aids in compliance. Many industries have regulations and standards that businesses must adhere to. Well-documented procedures provide evidence that the company is following these regulations, which can be crucial during audits or inspections.

Effective documentation practices involve creating clear, concise, and accessible documents. This might include using step-by-step instructions, visual aids like flowcharts or diagrams, and regular updates to ensure the procedures remain current. For example, a well-documented procedure for handling inventory might include detailed steps for receiving shipments, checking for accuracy, and updating inventory records, complete with diagrams showing the correct way to label and store items.

## THE IMPACT OF INTERNAL PROCESSES ON BUSINESS PERFORMANCE

The impact of internal processes on business performance is profound. When our processes are well-defined and meticulously followed, the benefits extend far beyond just operational efficiency. They touch every aspect of our business, from the quality of our products to the satisfaction of our employees.

Efficiency and productivity are among the most immediate benefits of well-defined processes. When everyone knows the exact steps needed to complete a task, operations run more smoothly. Tasks are completed faster, and there is less confusion and downtime. For example, a streamlined inventory management process ensures that stock levels are monitored accurately and replenished promptly, reducing the likelihood of stockouts or overstock situations. This reduction in redundancy and waste translates directly into cost savings and increased productivity.

Quality and consistency are also significantly enhanced through standardized processes. Having clear, established procedures ensures that every product or service meets the same high standards. This consistency is crucial for building and maintaining customer trust. If customers know they can expect the same quality every time they interact with our business, they are more likely to become repeat customers. For instance, a company in the food industry might implement strict quality control processes to ensure that every product leaving the factory is up to standard. By adhering to these processes, the company can consistently deliver high-quality products, thereby enhancing its reputation and customer loyalty.

A case study that illustrates this point involves a mid-sized manufacturing firm. This company struggled with inconsistent product quality, which led to customer complaints and returns. By implementing standardized processes for every stage of production—from raw material inspection to final product testing—they were able to achieve a remarkable turnaround. Quality issues decreased significantly, customer satisfaction improved, and the firm saw a reduction in waste and rework costs.

Employee satisfaction and engagement are also positively impacted by clear internal processes. When employees understand their roles and the steps they need to follow, they are less likely to feel frustrated or overwhelmed. Clear processes provide a sense of direction and purpose, which can boost morale and job satisfaction. Additionally, involving employees in the design and improvement of these processes fosters a sense of ownership and engagement. When employees feel that their input is valued and that they have a stake in the success of the business, they are more likely to be motivated and committed to their work.

Consider a service-oriented company that faced high employee turnover due to frustration with unclear job expectations and processes. By involving their staff in a thorough review and redesign of their internal procedures, the company was able to create more logical, user-friendly workflows. This reduced frustration and improved overall job satisfaction.

Employees felt heard and valued, leading to higher engagement levels and reduced turnover rates.

The impact of internal processes on business performance is multifaceted. Streamlined operations enhance efficiency and productivity; standardized procedures ensure quality and consistency, and clear, well-defined processes improve employee satisfaction and engagement. By focusing on refining our internal processes, we can achieve significant improvements in every aspect of our business, setting the stage for long-term success and sustainability.

## CHALLENGES IN MANAGING INTERNAL PROCESSES

Managing internal processes presents a variety of challenges that can impact our business's efficiency and overall performance. One of the most common issues is identifying and addressing bottlenecks. Bottlenecks occur when a particular stage in a process slows down the entire workflow, causing delays and reducing productivity. These can be difficult to spot, especially in complex operations where multiple tasks are interdependent. However, recognizing these slow points is crucial for streamlining our processes and maintaining smooth operations.

Managing process complexity and interdependencies is another significant challenge. As our business grows, our processes often become more intricate, with different departments and functions relying on each other to complete their tasks. This interdependence can lead to complications if one part of the process fails or lags behind, affecting the entire chain of operations. Keeping track of these complex relationships and ensuring that each component works harmoniously with the others is essential for maintaining efficiency and avoiding disruptions.

Additionally, keeping processes up to date with changing business needs is a constant challenge. The business environment is dynamic, with market conditions, customer expectations, and technological advancements evolving rapidly. Our processes need to be flexible enough to adapt to these changes without causing significant disruptions. This requires a proactive approach to continuously evaluate and update our processes to ensure they remain relevant and effective.

To overcome these challenges, we can employ several strategies. Effective process mapping and analysis are fundamental techniques. By visually mapping out our processes, we can gain a clear understanding of each step and how they interconnect. This helps us identify bottlenecks and areas for improvement more easily. Tools like flowcharts and process diagrams are invaluable for this purpose, providing a clear visual representation of our workflows.

Continuous process improvement methodologies, such as Lean and Six Sigma, offer structured approaches to refining our processes. These methodologies focus on eliminating waste, reducing variation, and improving quality. They provide a framework for systematically identifying and implementing improvements, helping us to enhance efficiency and effectiveness continually.

Leadership support and employee involvement are also crucial for successful process management. Leaders play a vital role in setting the tone and prioritizing process improvement initiatives. Their commitment and support can drive the necessary changes and allocate the required resources. On the other hand, involving employees in the process improvement efforts ensures that those who are directly engaged with the processes have a say in how they are designed and refined. Employees often have valuable insights into the practical aspects of the processes and can provide feedback that leads to more effective solutions.

For example, consider a company facing delays in its order fulfillment process. By mapping out the entire process, the team identified a bottleneck at the order processing stage, where manual data entry was causing delays. Implementing an automated system for order processing not only eliminated the bottleneck but also reduced errors and sped up the entire workflow. Leadership supported the initiative by providing the necessary resources for the automation project, and employees were involved in the selection and implementation of the new system, ensuring a smooth transition.

Managing internal processes involves addressing common issues like bottlenecks, complexity, and keeping processes current. By employing effective process mapping and analysis techniques, leveraging continuous improvement methodologies, and ensuring strong leadership support and employee involvement, we can overcome these challenges. This approach helps us maintain efficient, effective operations that can adapt to changing business needs, ultimately leading to sustained success.

## Conclusion

As we wrap up this chapter, it's important to reflect on the key points we've covered about managing and optimizing internal processes. We've explored how crucial these processes are for maintaining efficiency and consistency across our operations. Whether it's production, marketing, or customer service, having well-defined procedures in place ensures that tasks are completed accurately and on time.

We also discussed the various types of internal processes, including operational, management, and support processes, and how each plays a unique role in the overall functioning of our business. Operational processes are the day-to-day activities that directly impact our customers. Management processes guide our strategic decisions and performance evaluations, while support processes provide the necessary resources and infrastructure.

Understanding and optimizing these internal processes is not just beneficial—it's essential. Well-organized processes help us avoid bottlenecks, reduce waste, and improve overall productivity. They ensure that we can deliver high-quality products and services consistently, which in turn boosts customer satisfaction and loyalty. By continuously refining our processes, we can stay ahead of the competition and adapt to changing market demands.

I encourage you to apply the concepts and strategies we've discussed to your business operations. Start by mapping out your current processes to identify areas that need improvement. Involve your team in this effort, as they often have valuable insights and ideas. Use methodologies like Lean and Six Sigma to systematically refine your processes, and don't forget the importance of documentation and training to ensure everyone is on the same page.

Remember, process management is an ongoing journey. It requires regular review and adaptation to remain effective. Committing to continuous improvement can create a more efficient, responsive, and successful business. Embrace the changes, involve your team, and watch as your operations become more streamlined and your business thrives. The effort you put into understanding and optimizing your internal processes will pay off in the long run, leading to sustained growth and success.

# 2
# ANALYZING CURRENT PROCESSES

Analyzing current processes is crucial for any business aiming to improve its efficiency and effectiveness. Understanding how our operations work allows us to identify areas where we can make improvements, streamline activities, and eliminate waste. This analysis isn't just about spotting what's wrong; it's about recognizing what's right and building on those strengths. By thoroughly examining our processes, we can make informed decisions that lead to better performance and greater success.

In this chapter, we'll explore the importance of analyzing current processes and the benefits they bring to our business. We'll delve into process mapping, a vital tool that helps us visualize our workflows and understand each step's role and impact. We will discuss how to identify bottlenecks and inefficiencies, which are often the hidden culprits behind delays and increased costs. Understanding these issues allows us to target them directly and make the necessary adjustments.

We will also discuss the steps involved in conducting a process audit. This involves systematically examining our processes, gathering relevant data, and identifying areas for improvement. Through a case study, we will see how another company successfully used a process audit to enhance its operations, providing a practical example of the concepts in action.

The chapter will cover the importance of data in process analysis. We will discuss what types of data to collect and the tools available to help us gather and analyze this information. Accurate data collection is the backbone of any good analysis, providing the insights needed to make effective changes.

Engaging employees in the process analysis is another critical aspect we'll cover. Employees who work within these processes daily have invaluable insights and ideas. By involving them, we not only gain their expertise but also foster a sense of ownership and commitment to the improvements.

Developing actionable insights from our analysis is essential. It's not enough to identify problems; we need to create a clear action plan with specific goals, timelines, and assigned responsibilities. This ensures that the insights gained lead to real, tangible improvements.

Finally, we will discuss how to implement these process improvements effectively. Communicating changes, providing the necessary training and support, and monitoring the results are all crucial steps to ensure the success of our efforts. We will look at another case study to see how these steps were applied in a real-world scenario, highlighting the benefits achieved.

Analyzing our current processes is a vital step towards continuous improvement and operational excellence. By understanding and refining our workflows, we can create a more efficient, effective, and agile business capable of adapting to changes and seizing new opportunities. This chapter provides the tools and knowledge needed to embark on this journey, encouraging you to apply these concepts to enhance your own operations.

## UNDERSTANDING PROCESS MAPPING

Understanding process mapping is crucial for any business aiming to enhance its operations. Process mapping is essentially a method to visually document, analyze, and improve the steps involved in a business process. By creating a visual representation, we can see how work flows from start to finish, identifying each step, decision point, and interaction. This visualization helps us understand the current state of our processes, making it easier to spot inefficiencies and areas for improvement.

The importance of visualizing processes cannot be overstated. When we lay out a process visually, it becomes much clearer where bottlenecks occur, where resources are being wasted, and where there might be unnecessary steps. It allows everyone involved to have a shared understanding of how things work, which is crucial for effective communication and collaboration. A visual map can also help us ensure that everyone is following the same procedures, maintaining consistency across the board.

To get started with process mapping, we need to familiarize ourselves with some common tools and techniques. Flowcharts are probably the most well-known. They use symbols and arrows to represent different steps and the flow of work, making it easy to follow the sequence of activities. Another useful tool is the swimlane diagram, which organizes steps into lanes based on who is responsible for each part of the process. This is particularly helpful for processes that involve multiple departments or roles, as it clearly shows how tasks are divided and where handoffs occur.

Creating a process map begins with identifying the process we want to document. We gather all relevant information about the process, including inputs, outputs, and the sequence of activities. It's important to involve the people who are directly engaged in the process, as they can provide detailed insights and identify steps that might not be immediately obvious. Once we have all the information, we start by drawing the process from beginning to end, using the appropriate symbols and notations.

For example, let's say we are mapping our customer service process. We start with the initial customer inquiry, move through the various steps of logging the issue, assigning it to the right team member, resolving the issue, and finally closing the ticket and following up with the customer. Each of these steps would be represented visually, showing the flow of work and any decision points along the way.

Effective process maps are not just static documents; they should be used actively to drive improvements. Once we have our map, we can analyze it to identify inefficiencies, redundancies, and potential bottlenecks. We might notice, for instance, that too much time is spent on handoffs between departments or that certain steps could be automated to save time.

In summary, process mapping is a powerful tool for understanding and improving our business processes. By creating a visual representation of our workflows, we can gain valuable insights into how work gets done, identify areas for improvement, and ensure everyone is on the same page. This approach not only helps us streamline operations but also enhances communication and collaboration within our team. Whether we're using flowcharts, swimlane diagrams, or other mapping techniques, the goal is to make our processes as efficient and effective as possible, ultimately driving better business outcomes.

## IDENTIFYING BOTTLENECKS AND INEFFICIENCIES

Identifying bottlenecks and inefficiencies is crucial for improving any business process. A bottleneck is any point in a process where the flow of work slows down, causing delays and reducing overall efficiency. Inefficiencies, on the other hand, refer to any aspects of a process that waste time, resources, or effort. Both bottlenecks and inefficiencies can significantly impact productivity and the quality of output.

Bottlenecks can occur in various areas of a business. For instance, on a production line, a bottleneck might be a particular machine that operates slower than the rest, causing a backlog of work. In administrative processes, bottlenecks can arise when approval from a single individual is required before moving forward, leading to delays. In customer service, a bottleneck might occur if the response time to customer inquiries is slow due to an overloaded support team. Recognizing these typical areas is the first step toward addressing the issues.

Several techniques can be employed to effectively identify bottlenecks. One effective method is process observation and walkthroughs. By observing the process in action, we can see firsthand where delays occur and how workflows go from one step to the next. This hands-on approach provides a clear picture of the real-time challenges faced by the team.

Data analysis and performance metrics are also vital tools in identifying bottlenecks. By collecting and analyzing data on various aspects of the process, such as time taken for each step, error rates, and resource utilization, we can pinpoint where inefficiencies exist. Performance metrics, like cycle time and throughput, provide quantifiable insights that highlight areas needing improvement.

Employee feedback and interviews are equally important in identifying bottlenecks. The people who work within these processes daily often have the best insights into where problems lie. By involving employees and asking for their input, we gain a deeper understanding of the issues from their perspective. This collaborative approach not only helps identify bottlenecks but also fosters a culture of continuous improvement and engagement among staff.

For example, let's say we notice that our order fulfillment process is slower than expected. By observing the process, we might see that orders are piling up at the packing stage. Data analysis might reveal that the packing team is consistently slower due to a lack of sufficient packing materials or an inefficient packing setup. Through interviews, employees might share that the packing area is too small or that they often run out of necessary supplies. Armed with this information, we can make informed decisions about how to alleviate these bottlenecks, whether through reorganization, better supply management, or investing in additional resources.

Identifying bottlenecks and inefficiencies is not a one-time activity but an ongoing effort. As our business grows and processes evolve, new bottlenecks can emerge. Regularly revisiting and analyzing our processes ensures that we remain efficient and continue to improve. By using a combination of observation, data analysis, and employee feedback, we can effectively identify and address these issues, paving the way for smoother operations and better overall performance. This proactive approach helps maintain a high level of productivity and supports the long-term success of our business.

## CONDUCTING A PROCESS AUDIT

Conducting a process audit is a crucial step in identifying inefficiencies and opportunities for improvement within our business operations. It allows us to take a close look at our current processes, understand their effectiveness, and pinpoint areas that need attention. The audit process involves several key steps, each of which is vital for a comprehensive assessment.

The first step in conducting a process audit is planning and preparation. This phase involves defining the scope and objectives of the audit. We need to decide which processes will be audited, what specific aspects we are focusing on, and what outcomes we expect. Clear objectives help guide the audit and ensure that we cover all necessary areas. During this phase, it's also important to gather a team that will be responsible for conducting the audit. This team should include individuals who are familiar with the processes being audited and who can provide valuable insights.

Next, we move on to gathering and analyzing data. This step is critical, as accurate data provides the foundation for our audit findings. We collect data on various aspects of the process, such as time taken for each step, resources used, and any errors or delays encountered. This data can be gathered through observations, employee interviews, and reviewing existing records or reports. Once we have the data, we analyze it to identify patterns, bottlenecks, and inefficiencies. This analysis helps us understand where the process is breaking down and why.

After gathering and analyzing the data, the final step is documenting findings and insights. This involves compiling all the information into a clear and comprehensive report. The report should detail the current state of the process, high-lighting any issues or inefficiencies identified during the audit. It should also include recommendations for improvements based on the data analysis. Effective documentation is crucial because it provides a roadmap for implementing changes and allows us to track progress over time.

For example, consider a process audit conducted on our customer service operations. During the planning phase, we might decide to focus on the process of handling customer complaints, aiming to reduce response times and improve resolution rates. We would gather a team that includes customer service representatives and managers who are familiar with this process.

In the data-gathering phase, we would collect information on how long it takes to respond to complaints, the number of interactions required to resolve an issue, and any common delays or obstacles. This might involve reviewing customer service logs, observing the team at work, and conducting interviews with employees to understand their challenges.

Once we have this data, we analyze it to identify patterns. We might find that a significant delay occurs at the initial response stage because representatives are often busy with other tasks. We may also discover that certain types of complaints take longer to resolve due to a lack of clear guidelines.

In the final documentation phase, we compile these findings into a report. The report highlights the key issues, such as delayed initial responses and inconsistent handling of specific complaints. It also includes recommendations, such as assigning dedicated staff to handle complaints and creating standardized guidelines for common issues. This documentation serves as a blueprint for making improvements, helping us track our progress and ensure that the changes lead to better performance.

Conducting a process audit is an invaluable tool for improving our operations. By systematically planning, gathering and analyzing data, and documenting our findings, we can gain a clear understanding of our processes and make informed decisions to enhance efficiency and effectiveness. This structured approach not only helps address current issues but also sets the stage for ongoing improvement and success in our business.

## UTILIZING DATA FOR PROCESS ANALYSIS

Utilizing data for process analysis is essential for any business looking to improve its operations. Data serves as the backbone of process analysis, offering objective insights that help us understand how our processes are performing. By examining data, we can identify strengths and weaknesses, uncover trends, and make informed decisions that drive efficiency and effectiveness.

The importance of data in process analysis cannot be overstated. Data provides a clear, unbiased picture of what is happening within our processes. It helps us see beyond subjective impressions and anecdotes to understand the true performance of our operations. For instance, if we notice that a particular task is taking longer than expected, data can reveal whether this is an isolated incident or part of a broader trend. By collecting and analyzing the right types of data, we can pinpoint specific issues and opportunities for improvement.

When it comes to the types of data to collect, there are several key metrics to consider. Time-related data, such as the duration of each process step, is crucial for identifying bottlenecks and inefficiencies. Cost data helps us understand the financial impact of our processes, revealing areas where we might be overspending. Quality metrics, such as error rates or customer satisfaction scores, provide insights into the effectiveness of our processes and highlight areas where improvements are needed.

To collect and analyze this data effectively, we have a variety of tools at our disposal. Surveys and questionnaires are useful for gathering qualitative data from employees and customers. They can provide valuable insights into how processes are perceived and where they might be falling short. Time-tracking software allows us to measure how long different tasks and activities take, helping us identify delays and inefficiencies. Performance dashboards offer a comprehensive view of our process metrics, presenting data in a clear and accessible format that makes it easy to spot trends and anomalies.

Analyzing process data involves applying specific techniques to interpret the information and draw meaningful conclusions. Pareto analysis is a useful method for identifying the most significant factors affecting our processes. By focusing on the "vital few" causes that contribute to most problems, we can prioritize our improvement efforts for maximum impact. Root cause analysis helps us delve deeper into the underlying issues that are driving process inefficiencies. By identifying the root causes, we can develop targeted solutions that address the problem at its source.

For example, let's say we are examining our order fulfillment process. By collecting time-related data, we discover that the packing stage consistently takes longer than anticipated. Using root cause analysis, we might find that this delay is due to frequent shortages of packing materials, requiring staff to spend time sourcing supplies instead of packing orders. Armed with this insight, we can implement a more reliable inventory management system for packing materials, ensuring they are always available when needed.

Utilizing data for process analysis is a powerful way to understand and improve our operations. By collecting the right types of data and using effective tools and techniques for analysis, we can gain valuable insights into our processes and make informed decisions that enhance efficiency, reduce costs, and improve quality. This data-driven approach enables us to continuously refine our operations, ensuring that we remain competitive and capable of meeting the evolving needs of our business and customers.

## ENGAGING EMPLOYEES IN PROCESS ANALYSIS

Engaging employees in process analysis is essential for gaining a comprehensive understanding of our business operations. Employees are on the front lines, interacting with processes daily, and their insights can be invaluable. When we involve them in analyzing these processes, we not only tap into their firsthand knowledge but also foster a sense of ownership and commitment to any improvements we decide to implement.

The benefits of involving employees in process analysis are significant. First, employees can provide practical insights that might not be evident from data alone. They understand the nuances of the processes they work with and can often point out inefficiencies or bottlenecks that might be overlooked. Second, involving employees in the analysis fosters a culture of collaboration and continuous improvement. When employees see that their input is valued, they are more likely to engage with the process and contribute meaningful suggestions. This involvement also increases their commitment to any changes made, as they feel a sense of ownership over the improvements.

Encouraging employee participation can be achieved through various techniques. Open communication is key. We need to create an environment where employees feel comfortable sharing their thoughts and experiences without fear of criticism. Regular meetings and feedback sessions can help facilitate this open dialogue. Additionally, providing incentives for valuable contributions can motivate employees to participate actively. Recognition programs, such as employee of the month or small rewards for useful suggestions, can also boost participation.

Effectively gathering employee input requires a structured approach. Surveys and questionnaires are useful tools for collecting broad feedback from a large group of employees. These instruments can be designed to gather specific information about different aspects of the processes, allowing us to identify common themes and issues. They provide a way for employees to share their thoughts anonymously, which can lead to more honest and open feedback.

Focus groups and workshops offer a more interactive method for gathering input. In these sessions, employees can discuss their experiences and ideas in a group setting, allowing for a dynamic exchange of perspectives. This format encourages brainstorming and can lead to innovative solutions that might not emerge in more structured settings. Workshops also provide an opportunity for employees to collaborate directly on process improvements, fostering a sense of teamwork and shared purpose.

One-on-one interviews are another effective method for gathering detailed feedback. These interviews allow for deeper exploration of specific issues and provide a platform for employees to share their insights in a more personal and focused manner. They are particularly useful for understanding the context behind certain inefficiencies and for uncovering root causes that might not be apparent from survey data.

For example, if we are looking to improve our customer service process, we might start with a survey to gather general feedback on areas such as response times, common issues, and overall satisfaction. We could then hold focus groups with customer service representatives to dive deeper into these areas and explore potential solutions collaboratively. Finally, one-on-one interviews with team members who handle specific aspects of customer service could provide detailed insights into particular challenges and opportunities for improvement.

Engaging employees in process analysis is a powerful way to enhance our understanding of business operations and drive meaningful improvements. By involving employees through surveys, focus groups, and interviews, we tap into their valuable insights and foster a culture of continuous improvement. This collaborative approach leads to better processes and increases employee satisfaction and engagement, ultimately contributing to the success of our business.

## DEVELOPING ACTIONABLE INSIGHTS

Developing actionable insights is a critical step in transforming the raw data and observations from our process analysis into concrete improvements. This stage is where we take the findings from our analysis and decide how to use them to enhance our operations.

Interpreting analysis results involves carefully examining the data to identify key findings. This means looking for patterns, trends, and anomalies that reveal underlying issues in our processes. For example, we might notice that certain steps consistently take longer than others, indicating a potential bottleneck. We also need to pay attention to feedback from employees, as their insights can highlight practical challenges and inefficiencies that data alone might not fully capture.

Once we've identified the key findings, the next step is to prioritize areas for improvement. Not all issues can or should be addressed at once. We need to evaluate which problems have the most significant impact on our operations and which improvements will deliver the greatest benefits. This prioritization helps us focus our efforts and resources on the most critical areas, ensuring that we achieve meaningful and sustainable improvements.

Creating an action plan is essential for turning our insights into results. This plan should start with setting clear objectives and goals. What do we want to achieve with our improvements? These goals should be specific, measurable, attainable, relevant, and time-bound (SMART). For instance, if our goal is to reduce the time it takes to process customer orders, we need to specify the target time and the deadline for achieving this improvement.

Developing a timeline and milestones is the next part of the action plan. This involves breaking down the overall goal into smaller, manageable steps and setting deadlines for each. A timeline helps keep the project on track and ensures that everyone involved knows what needs to be done and by when. Milestones serve as checkpoints along the way, allowing us to monitor progress and adjust as needed.

Assigning responsibilities and resources is crucial for ensuring that the action plan is executed effectively. Each task or milestone should have a designated owner who is accountable for its completion. This clarity helps prevent confusion and ensures that all aspects of the plan are addressed. Additionally, we need to allocate the necessary resources, whether it's personnel, budget, or tools, to support the execution of the plan. Without adequate resources, even the best-laid plans can falter.

For example, let's say our analysis revealed that our customer support response times are longer than desired. Our key finding might be that a lack of clear guidelines and inconsistent training are causing delays. We prioritize this issue because it directly impacts customer satisfaction. Our objective is to reduce response times by 50 percent within three months. We develop a timeline that includes revising training materials, conducting training sessions, and implementing a new support ticketing system, with milestones at each phase. We assign the customer service manager to lead this initiative and allocate funds for the new software and training resources.

Developing actionable insights involves interpreting analysis results to identify key findings and prioritizing areas for improvement. Creating an action plan with clear objectives, a timeline, milestones, and assigned responsibilities ensures that these insights lead to real, tangible improvements. By following this structured approach, we can enhance our processes, boost efficiency, and drive our business toward greater success.

## Implementing Process Improvements

Implementing process improvements is a critical step in enhancing the efficiency and effectiveness of our operations. Once we have identified the areas that need improvement and developed an actionable plan, the next challenge is to execute these changes smoothly.

One of the most important strategies for implementing changes is communicating them effectively to the team. Clear and open communication is essential for ensuring everyone understands the reasons for the changes, what the changes entail, and how they will benefit the organization. This helps to alleviate any concerns or resistance from employees who might be apprehensive about altering their routines. We need to explain the benefits of the new processes and how they will make the team's work more efficient and productive. Regular updates and open forums for questions and feedback can help keep everyone informed and engaged throughout the transition.

Providing training and support is another crucial aspect of implementing process improvements. Even the best-designed processes can fail if employees do not know how to execute them correctly. Comprehensive training sessions should be organized to ensure that everyone is comfortable with the new procedures. This might include hands-on workshops, instructional videos, and detailed manuals. Additionally, ongoing support should be available to help employees as they adapt to the new processes. This support can come in the form of a help desk, dedicated team members who can assist with questions, or regular check-ins to address any issues that arise.

Monitoring and adjusting the new processes as needed is the final step in ensuring successful implementation. It's essential to keep a close eye on how the new processes are performing and to gather feedback from employees who are using them daily. This allows us to identify any unforeseen issues or areas where further adjustments might be necessary. Regular performance metrics and feedback loops can help track the success of the improvements and highlight any areas that need fine-tuning. Being open to making adjustments based on real-world feedback ensures that the new processes continue to meet our goals and improve our operations.

For example, let's say we've decided to implement a new inventory management system to reduce errors and streamline the process. First, we communicate the change to our team, explaining how the new system will reduce manual errors and save time. We outline the steps of the implementation and provide a timeline. Next, we organize training sessions where employees can learn how to use the new system with hands-on practice and support from experts. After the system goes live, we monitor its performance closely, checking inventory accuracy rates and gathering feedback from the team. If issues arise, such as difficulties with certain features, we make the necessary adjustments and continue to provide support.

Implementing process improvements requires clear communication, thorough training and support, and ongoing monitoring and adjustments. By following these strategies, we can ensure that the new processes are adopted smoothly and that they deliver the intended benefits. This approach not only enhances our operations but also fosters a culture of continuous improvement where the team feels supported and empowered to embrace change.

## Conclusion

This chapter discussed how vital it is to regularly examine our business processes to identify inefficiencies and areas for enhancement. Understanding these processes in detail allows us to make informed decisions that can significantly boost our operational efficiency and overall effectiveness.

We also explored various tools and techniques for process analysis, such as process mapping, data collection, and employee feedback. These methods provide a comprehensive understanding of how our processes work and where they might be falling short. By using these tools, we can pinpoint bottlenecks and inefficiencies that hinder our productivity and address them systematically.

The goal of this chapter was not just to provide information but to inspire you to take action. Conducting a thorough process analysis in your own organization can uncover opportunities for improvement that might otherwise remain hidden. It's an investment of time and effort that can pay off significantly in terms of enhanced efficiency, reduced costs, and improved employee satisfaction.

Remember, the process of improvement doesn't stop once initial changes are made. Continuous process improvement is an ongoing journey. By regularly revisiting and refining your processes, you can keep your business agile and responsive to changing conditions. This commitment to continuous improvement fosters a culture of excellence and innovation, ensuring that your organization remains competitive and capable of meeting its goals.

I encourage you to apply the concepts and strategies we've discussed. Start by analyzing your current processes, involve your team in identifying issues and opportunities, and implement targeted improvements. The benefits of these efforts will be evident in smoother operations, better resource utilization, and a more motivated and engaged workforce. Embrace the challenge of continuous improvement, and you will see your business thrive and grow.

# 3

# DESIGNING EFFECTIVE PROCESSES

Designing effective processes is essential for any business. Well-designed processes create a foundation for efficiency, consistency, and growth. They help ensure that tasks are completed correctly and on time, allowing the business to operate smoothly and meet its goals. In this chapter, we will explore the steps involved in designing effective processes, from establishing clear objectives to involving stakeholders and setting measurable targets. By the end of this chapter, you'll have a comprehensive understanding of how to create processes that enhance your business operations.

## ESTABLISHING OBJECTIVES

First, let's talk about establishing objectives. It's crucial to start by defining clear process goals. These goals should align with your overall business objectives to ensure that every process contributes to your broader mission. For example, if one of your business goals is to improve customer satisfaction, your process goals might include reducing response times and increasing the accuracy of customer orders. Setting measurable targets for each goal is equally important. Measurable targets provide a way to track progress and determine whether the process is successful. They give your team a clear idea of what they are working towards and allow you to make data-driven decisions.

## INVOLVING STAKEHOLDERS

Involving stakeholders is another critical aspect of designing effective processes. Stakeholders are individuals or groups who have a vested interest in the process, such as employees, managers, and customers. Identifying these key stakeholders early on ensures that you consider their needs and perspectives when designing the process. Involving them in the design phase helps build buy-in and increases the likelihood of successful implementation. Techniques for gathering stakeholder input can vary, from surveys and interviews to workshops and brainstorming sessions. The goal is to collect a wide range of insights and feedback to create a process that meets everyone's needs.

For example, when designing a new customer service process, it's beneficial to gather input from frontline employees who interact with customers daily. They can provide valuable insights into common issues and suggest practical solutions. Similarly, involving customers by seeking their feedback on service improvements can help ensure that the new process enhances their experience.

## DEVELOPING PROCESS FLOW

Developing a process flow is a critical part of designing effective processes. It involves creating a clear visual representation of each step involved in a task or series of tasks. This helps everyone understand how work should be done and where improvements can be made.

The first step in designing a process flow is to outline the major steps involved in the process. Start by identifying the beginning and end points. Then, map out each step that takes you from start to finish. It's important to be as detailed as possible to capture all the necessary actions. For example, if you're mapping out a customer order process, include everything from receiving the order to delivering the product.

Next, you'll want to use tools to create process flow diagrams. Flowcharts and process maps are particularly useful for this. Flowcharts use shapes and arrows to show the process's sequence of steps and decisions. Process maps, on the other hand, provide a broader view of how different processes interact with each other. Both tools help visualize the flow of work, making it easier to identify bottlenecks and areas for improvement.

Documenting each step in the process is crucial. Without proper documentation, it's easy for details to get lost or misunderstood. Clear documentation serves as a reference guide for everyone involved. It ensures consistency and provides a basis for training new employees. When documenting, describe each step in simple, straightforward language. Include any necessary details, such as who is responsible for each task, what resources are needed, and any relevant timelines.

For instance, when I worked on improving our order fulfillment process, we started by sketching out the major steps on a whiteboard. We then used a flowchart tool to create a more detailed diagram. This visual aid helped us see that our inventory check was a major bottleneck. By documenting the steps involved in this task, we identified unnecessary actions and streamlined the process.

Having a detailed process flow is beneficial for several reasons. It provides clarity, ensuring everyone understands their role and how their work fits into the bigger picture. It also makes it easier to spot inefficiencies and make improvements.

31

Regularly reviewing and updating the process flow helps keep the process efficient and aligned with any changes in the business.

## STANDARDIZING PROCEDURES

Standardizing procedures is a cornerstone of efficient business operations. One effective way to achieve this is by creating Standard Operating Procedures (SOPs). SOPs are detailed, written instructions that describe exactly how to perform a task. They ensure that everyone in the organization is on the same page and follows the same steps, leading to consistency and reliability.

When creating SOPs, it's important to be clear and specific. Start by identifying the task that needs a procedure. Break it down into each individual step, and write these steps in simple, straightforward language. The goal is to make the SOP easy to follow so that any employee, regardless of their experience level, can understand and execute the task correctly. Including details such as the necessary tools or materials, the responsible personnel, and the expected outcomes can also be helpful.

The benefits of standardization through SOPs are numerous. First, it promotes consistency. When everyone follows the same procedures, the quality of work is maintained at a high level. This is particularly important in areas like production, where variability can lead to defects and customer dissatisfaction. For example, in a bakery, having a standardized recipe and baking procedure ensures that each loaf of bread is of the same quality every time.

Efficiency is another significant benefit. SOPs eliminate the guesswork, allowing tasks to be completed more quickly and with fewer errors. Employees don't waste time figuring out how to do something because the instructions are right there. This streamlined approach saves time and reduces the likelihood of mistakes. For example, a well-documented SOP for handling common inquiries can speed up response times and improve customer satisfaction in a customer service department.

SOPs also play a crucial role in training new employees. With clear, written procedures, new hires can learn their tasks more quickly and confidently. Instead of relying solely on verbal instructions or on-the-job training, they have a concrete reference to guide them. This can reduce the training period and help new employees become productive team members sooner. For instance, in a retail store, an SOP detailing the steps for opening and closing the store can help new employees learn the routine without constant supervision.

One example of a well-documented SOP could be a procedure for handling inventory in a warehouse. The SOP might include steps for receiving shipments, checking for damage, updating inventory records, and storing items in the correct locations. Each step would be described in detail, with any necessary forms or checklists included as attachments. This ensures that all employees follow the same process, reducing errors and improving inventory accuracy.

## IMPLEMENTING AUTOMATION

Implementing automation in a business can significantly enhance efficiency and productivity. The first step is identifying areas suitable for automation. These are usually tasks that are repetitive, time-consuming, and prone to human error. For instance, data entry, payroll processing, and inventory management are often good candidates for automation. By closely examining the workflows in your business, you can pinpoint which tasks take up the most time and are most susceptible to mistakes.

The benefits of automation are substantial. For one, it reduces manual errors. Humans are prone to making mistakes, especially when performing monotonous tasks. Automation ensures that these tasks are done accurately every time. This improves the quality of work and frees employees to focus on more strategic, value-added activities. Increased speed is another major benefit. Automated processes can be completed much faster than manual ones, leading to quicker turnaround times and increased overall productivity. For example, automating the invoice processing system can significantly reduce the time it takes to manage accounts payable, leading to faster payments and improved cash flow.

Various tools and technologies are available for process automation. Software solutions like ERP (Enterprise Resource Planning) systems integrate various business processes into a single system, making managing and automating tasks easier. For example, an ERP system can automate everything from order processing to inventory management, ensuring that these tasks are completed efficiently and accurately. Robotic Process Automation (RPA) is another powerful tool that uses software robots to perform routine tasks. These robots can mimic human actions, such as entering data or processing transactions, and are particularly useful for tasks that require interacting with multiple systems.

To illustrate, imagine a retail business that struggles with managing inventory manually. The process is slow, error-prone, and takes up a significant amount of employees' time. By implementing inventory management software, the business can automate tracking stock levels, reorder products when they run low, and generate real-time reports. This not only reduces the risk of stockouts or overstock but also allows employees to focus on more critical tasks like customer service and sales.

Similarly, a financial services firm can use RPA to automate compliance reporting. This task involves gathering data from various sources, verifying its accuracy, and compiling reports, which is tedious and time-consuming. By using RPA, the firm can ensure that the data is collected and processed quickly and accurately, reducing the risk of non-compliance and allowing employees to focus on more analytical tasks.

In summary, implementing automation involves identifying suitable areas, understanding the benefits, and choosing the right tools and technologies. By automating repetitive and error-prone tasks, businesses can improve accuracy, speed up processes, and free up valuable employee time for more strategic activities. This leads to a more efficient, productive, and ultimately successful operation.

## TESTING AND REFINING PROCESSES

Testing and refining processes is crucial for ensuring they work as intended before fully implementing them across the business. Pilot testing new processes is essential because it allows us to identify potential issues and adjust in a controlled environment. By testing on a small scale, we can see how the process performs and gather valuable insights without risking large-scale disruptions.

One effective technique for testing process effectiveness is conducting simulations. Simulations allow us to model the process in a virtual environment, enabling us to see how it performs under different conditions. This can help us identify potential bottlenecks, inefficiencies, or unforeseen problems. For instance, if we're introducing a new inventory management system, we can simulate various scenarios, such as peak order periods or supply chain disruptions, to see how the system handles them.

Another approach is to implement the process on a small scale within a specific department or for a limited time. This allows us to observe the process in action and gather real-world data on its performance. For example, if we're rolling out a new customer service protocol, we might start with one team or a subset of customers to see how well it works. This way, we can adjust based on actual experiences before implementing it company-wide.

Gathering feedback during this testing phase is critical. It's important to involve the employees who are directly affected by the new process, as they can provide valuable insights into its effectiveness and any issues they encounter. Encourage open and honest feedback, and take the time to listen to their concerns and suggestions. This feedback can help us fine-tune the process and address any problems before full implementation.

Once we've gathered feedback, making the necessary adjustments is the next step. This might involve tweaking specific steps, re-allocating resources, or even rethinking the process entirely. The goal is to refine the process until it runs smoothly and efficiently. By addressing issues early on, we can avoid larger problems down the road and ensure a successful implementation.

For instance, when we introduced a new sales process, we started with a small pilot program involving just a few sales reps. We simulated various sales scenarios and then implemented the process for a month. During this period, we collected feedback from the reps, which highlighted certain steps that were confusing or time-consuming. Based on their input, we made several adjustments, simplifying some steps and providing additional training where needed. This refinement made the final rollout much smoother and more effective.

## TRAINING AND COMMUNICATION

Training and communication are crucial when introducing new processes in a business. Training employees on new processes ensures that everyone understands their roles and responsibilities. It minimizes confusion and errors, leading to a smoother transition and more effective implementation. Even the best-designed processes can fail without proper training because employees are unsure how to execute them correctly.

Developing effective training programs involves several key elements. First, it's important to create clear, comprehensive training materials. These should include step-by-step instructions, visual aids, and examples that illustrate how the new process works. Hands-on training sessions can also be very beneficial, allowing employees to practice the new process in a controlled environment where they can ask questions and receive immediate feedback.

Additionally, ongoing support is essential. Employees should know whom to turn to if they encounter issues or have questions after the initial training. Providing a feedback loop where employees can share their experiences and suggestions for improvement can also enhance the training program.

Communicating process changes to the team requires a thoughtful approach. Start by clearly explaining why the change is necessary and how it will benefit the business and employees. Transparency is key; people are more likely to embrace change if they understand the reasons behind it. Use multiple communication channels, such as meetings, emails, and internal newsletters, to ensure everyone receives the information. Consistent messaging helps reinforce the importance of the new process and encourages compliance.

## MEASURING AND MONITORING PERFORMANCE

Measuring and monitoring performance is the next critical step. Establishing key performance indicators (KPIs) allows us to track the effectiveness of the new process. KPIs should be specific, measurable, and aligned with the business's overall goals. For instance, if we've implemented a new customer service protocol, KPIs might include response times, customer satisfaction scores, and the number of resolved issues.

We can use various techniques to monitor process performance. Dashboards provide a visual representation of KPIs, making it easy to see how the process is performing at a glance. Regular reviews, such as weekly or monthly meetings, allow us to discuss progress, identify any issues, and make necessary adjustments. These reviews should involve team members who are directly affected by the process, as their insights are invaluable for understanding how well the process works in practice.

Continuous improvement and regular updates are essential for maintaining the effectiveness of any process. The business environment is constantly changing, and processes need to adapt to these changes. Regularly soliciting feedback from employees and reviewing performance data helps us identify areas for improvement. Making incremental adjustments based on this feedback ensures that the process remains efficient and effective over time.

For example, when we rolled out a new sales process, we trained our sales team thoroughly, using a mix of instructional materials and hands-on practice. We communicated the change through multiple channels, ensuring everyone understood the reasons for the new process. After implementation, we monitored key metrics such as sales conversion rates and customer feedback. Regular review meetings helped us identify and address any issues, leading to continuous process improvement.

## CONCLUSION

Designing effective processes is essential for the smooth operation and success of any business. Well-structured processes ensure that tasks are completed consistently and efficiently, minimizing errors and maximizing productivity. When we take the time to design our processes thoughtfully, we set our business up for success by creating a strong foundation for growth and adaptability.

It's crucial to continuously evaluate and improve these processes. The business environment is always changing, and what works today might not be as effective tomorrow. Regularly reviewing our processes helps us stay ahead of the curve, allowing us to make adjustments before small issues become big problems. This ongoing evaluation ensures that our processes remain relevant and efficient, adapting to new challenges and opportunities.

The benefits of well-designed processes are clear. They lead to greater efficiency, higher quality outputs, and improved employee satisfaction. When everyone knows what is expected of them and has the tools they need to do their jobs well, the entire organization runs more smoothly. Customers notice the difference, too, appreciating the consistent quality and reliability that come from a well-oiled operation.

In the end, investing in process design and improvement is investing in the future success of our business. It's about creating an environment where efficiency and quality are the norms, not the exceptions. By committing to this approach, we can build a business that not only survives but thrives in a competitive marketplace.

# 4

# IMPLEMENTING NEW
# PROCEDURES

Effectively implementing new procedures is crucial for any business looking to improve its operations and stay competitive. When new procedures are rolled out without proper planning and communication, they can cause confusion and disrupt workflows. On the other hand, a well-executed implementation can lead to significant improvements in efficiency, consistency, and overall performance.

This chapter will discuss the steps necessary to ensure a smooth implementation of new procedures. We'll cover everything from planning and communication to training and support. By the end of this chapter, you should have a solid understanding of how to introduce new procedures in a way that minimizes disruption and maximizes benefits.

## PLANNING FOR IMPLEMENTATION

Planning for implementation is the first and perhaps most critical step. It starts with setting clear objectives and goals for the new procedures. This means understanding exactly what you want to achieve and how the new procedures will help you get there. Clear goals provide a roadmap for the entire implementation process and ensure everyone involved knows what success looks like.

Once the objectives are clear, it's important to identify the resources needed to implement the new procedures. This includes personnel, technology, and budget. Knowing what resources are required helps allocate them efficiently and ensures no surprises down the line. For instance, if new software is needed, it's crucial to budget for it and ensure that the necessary technology infrastructure is in place.

Developing a detailed implementation plan is the next step. This plan should outline each phase of the implementation process, complete with timelines and milestones. A well-thought-out plan acts as a guide, helping to keep the implementation on track and ensuring that nothing is overlooked. Timelines keep the process moving forward and prevent unnecessary delays, while milestones provide checkpoints to measure progress and make adjustments as needed.

For example, when we decided to implement a new inventory management system, we began by clearly defining our goals. We wanted to reduce stock discrepancies, improve order fulfillment times, and increase overall inventory accuracy. We then identified the resources we needed: a new software platform, training for our staff, and a budget to cover these costs. With these elements in place, we developed a detailed plan that included specific tasks, deadlines, and key milestones to track our progress.

Effectively implementing new procedures requires careful planning and clear communication. By setting clear objectives, identifying necessary resources, and developing a detailed implementation plan, you can ensure a smoother transition and achieve the desired improvements in your business operations. The next sections will dive deeper into each of these steps, providing practical advice and strategies to help you succeed.

## Communicating Changes

Effectively communicating changes in procedures is essential to ensure everyone in the organization understands what is happening and why. Clear and concise messages are key. When introducing new procedures, it's important to explain the changes in simple terms, highlighting the benefits and how they align with the company's goals. Avoid jargon and complex explanations; instead, focus on the practical aspects that directly impact employees' daily tasks.

Choosing the right communication channels is also crucial. Different channels work better for different types of messages and audiences. For significant announcements, holding a company-wide meeting can be effective, as it allows for direct interaction and immediate feedback. Emails are great for detailed instructions and documentation, ensuring everyone has a written reference. Intranet postings can serve as a central hub for all related information and are accessible anytime. By using a mix of these channels, you can reach everyone in the organization effectively.

Addressing employee concerns and questions is another important aspect of communication. Changes can be unsettling, and it's natural for employees to have questions or feel uncertain. Creating an open environment where employees feel comfortable voicing their concerns is essential. Regular Q&A sessions, feedback forms, and open-door policies can help. Providing clear and honest answers helps build trust and ensures that employees feel heard and valued.

## Training and Support

Training and support are critical for the successful implementation of new procedures. Developing comprehensive training programs ensures that all employees understand the new procedures and how to execute them correctly. Training should be thorough and practical, using real-life scenarios to demonstrate how the new procedures work.

Scheduling training sessions and workshops is an effective way to ensure everyone receives the necessary instruction. These sessions should be well-planned and spaced out to allow employees to absorb the information and practice the new procedures. Hands-on workshops can be particularly useful, as they allow employees to learn by doing and to ask questions in real time.

Providing ongoing support and resources is essential to reinforce the training. This can include FAQs, help desks, and easy access to documentation. An FAQ section can address common questions and concerns, providing quick answers. A help desk or dedicated support team can offer personalized assistance, helping employees troubleshoot any issues they encounter as they adapt to the new procedures.

For instance, when we implemented a new project management system, we crafted clear messages explaining why we were making the change and how it would benefit our workflow. We used a mix of meetings, emails, and intranet posts to communicate the changes. To address concerns, we held Q&A sessions where employees could ask questions and get immediate feedback. We then developed a comprehensive training program, including several hands-on workshops. After the initial training, we provided ongoing support through an FAQ section on our intranet and a dedicated help desk to assist with any issues.

## PILOT TESTING

Pilot testing is a crucial step in implementing new procedures. It allows us to test the new processes on a smaller scale before a full-scale rollout. Selecting the right pilot group for initial implementation is key. Ideally, this group should be representative of the larger organization and include individuals who are open to change and capable of providing valuable feedback. This group serves as a microcosm, helping us identify any issues or challenges that might arise during the broader implementation.

Once the pilot group is selected, we need to closely monitor their performance and gather their feedback. This involves regular check-ins, performance reviews, and open forums where the pilot group can share their experiences. It's important to listen to their input carefully, as they are on the front lines and can offer insights that we might not have considered. Their feedback helps us understand how the new procedures work in practice and highlights any areas that need improvement.

Based on the feedback and performance data from the pilot group, we can make necessary adjustments to the new procedures. This might involve tweaking certain steps, providing additional training, or addressing unforeseen challenges. The goal is to refine the procedures so that they are as effective and efficient as possible before the full rollout.

## FULL-SCALE IMPLEMENTATION

After making these adjustments, we move to full-scale implementation. This is the stage where we roll out the new procedures across the entire organization. It's crucial to ensure that all employees are informed and trained on the new processes. Clear communication and comprehensive training are essential to minimize confusion and ensure a smooth transition. Every employee should understand the new procedures, why they are being implemented, and how they will benefit the organization.

Setting up support systems is another critical component of full-scale implementation. Even with thorough training, questions and issues are bound to arise. Having a robust support system in place ensures that employees have the resources they need to address any problems quickly. This might include a dedicated help desk, an FAQ section, or regular support meetings. These resources provide employees with the confidence and support they need to adapt to the new procedures.

For example, when we introduced a new customer relationship management (CRM) system, we started with a pilot group of sales representatives. We monitored their use of the new system, gathered their feedback, and made several adjustments based on their experiences. Once we were confident that the system was functioning well, we rolled it out to the entire sales team. We provided comprehensive training sessions and set up a help desk to address any questions or issues that arose. This approach ensured a smooth transition and helped the entire team adapt to the new system effectively.

## Monitoring and Evaluation

Monitoring and evaluation are crucial steps in ensuring the success of new procedures. To measure success, we first establish key performance indicators (KPIs). These KPIs serve as benchmarks, helping us understand whether the new procedures are achieving the desired outcomes. They should be specific, measurable, and aligned with the overall goals of the business. For instance, if we're implementing a new sales process, KPIs might include the number of new leads generated, the conversion rate, and customer satisfaction scores.

Once we have our KPIs in place, it's important to regularly review performance data and gather feedback from employees. This helps us keep a pulse on how well the new procedures are working and where there might be room for improvement. Performance data provides an objective look at the results, while employee feedback offers insights into how the procedures are being implemented on the ground. Combining these perspectives gives us a comprehensive view of the process.

Based on our evaluations, we make continuous improvements to the procedures. This is an ongoing cycle of assessing performance, identifying areas for enhancement, and adjusting. It's important to remain flexible and responsive, as even well-designed processes can benefit from tweaks and refinements over time. Continuous improvement helps ensure that the procedures stay relevant and effective as the business environment evolves.

## OVERCOMING CHALLENGES

Overcoming challenges is an inherent part of implementing new procedures. Common challenges include resistance to change, lack of understanding, and inadequate resources. Identifying these challenges early on allows us to address them proactively. Resistance to change is often the biggest hurdle. Employees might be comfortable with the old way of doing things and wary of new processes. To address this, we need to communicate the benefits of the new procedures clearly and involve employees in the process. This can help them feel more invested and less resistant to the changes.

Ensuring leadership support and involvement is also crucial. When leaders actively support and participate in the implementation of new procedures, it sends a strong message to the rest of the organization. Leadership can help drive the change by modeling the desired behaviors and providing the necessary resources and support. This can include everything from approving budgets for new technology to participating in training sessions alongside employees.

For example, during the implementation of a new project management system, we faced some resistance from team members who were accustomed to the old system. By involving them in the pilot testing phase and incorporating their feedback into the final rollout, we were able to ease their concerns. Regular meetings with leadership helped reinforce the importance of the new system and ensured that everyone had the resources they needed to make the transition smoothly.

## Conclusion

Careful planning and execution are the cornerstones of successfully implementing new procedures. Without a well-thought-out plan, even the most beneficial changes can lead to confusion and disruption. When we take the time to clearly define our objectives, identify the necessary resources, and communicate effectively with our team, we set the stage for a smooth transition. Each step, from pilot testing to full-scale implementation, plays a crucial role in ensuring that the new procedures are adopted successfully and deliver the intended benefits.

It's equally important to remain flexible and responsive to feedback throughout this process. No plan is perfect, and unforeseen challenges are bound to arise. By actively seeking feedback from employees and regularly reviewing performance data, we can make necessary adjustments and improvements. This iterative approach helps us refine the procedures, making them more effective and ensuring they meet the needs of the organization.

Successful implementation of new procedures offers numerous benefits for organizational growth and efficiency. Well-designed and properly executed processes lead to increased productivity, reduced errors, and higher employee satisfaction. When everyone knows what is expected of them and has the tools they need to succeed, the entire organization runs more smoothly. Customers notice the difference, too, benefiting from consistent quality and reliable service.

The effort we put into planning, executing, and continuously improving new procedures pays off in the long run. It strengthens our operations and positions us for sustained growth. By staying flexible and responsive to feedback, we can ensure that our processes evolve with the changing needs of our business. The result is a more efficient, effective, and resilient organization.

# 5

## MONITORING AND
## EVALUATING PROCESSES

Monitoring and evaluating processes is essential for the long-term success of any business. It ensures that our operations are running smoothly and efficiently, allowing us to identify areas for improvement and make necessary adjustments. By closely monitoring our processes, we can catch issues early, refine our methods, and ultimately enhance our overall performance. This chapter will guide you through the critical aspects of monitoring and evaluating processes, including establishing key performance indicators (KPIs), collecting and analyzing data, and ensuring accuracy and reliability in our data collection efforts.

### ESTABLISHING KEY PERFORMANCE INDICATORS (KPIS)

Establishing key performance indicators (KPIs) is the first step in this process. KPIs are specific metrics that help us measure the success of our processes. They provide a clear and quantifiable way to assess performance and determine whether we are meeting our goals. The purpose of KPIs is to give us a snapshot of how well our processes are functioning and where we might need to make changes.

When selecting KPIs, choosing ones that are relevant and meaningful to our business is important. Effective KPIs should be specific, measurable, attainable, relevant, and time-bound. For example, in a sales process, common KPIs might include the number of new leads generated, the conversion rate, and customer satisfaction scores. In manufacturing, KPIs might focus on production efficiency, defect rates, and on-time delivery.

## Data Collection and Analysis

Collecting and analyzing process performance data is the next crucial step. There are various methods for gathering this data, ranging from manual tracking to automated systems. The key is to ensure that the data we collect is accurate and reliable. Inaccurate data can lead to misguided decisions and ineffective improvements. Using tools and technologies designed for data analysis can help streamline this process and provide more precise insights.

For instance, we might use software that tracks production metrics in real time, allowing us to see immediately if there are any delays or issues. Similarly, customer relationship management (CRM) systems can provide detailed reports on sales activities, helping us understand where our sales process might be falling short.

Accuracy and reliability in data collection cannot be overstated. If our data is flawed, our evaluations and subsequent decisions will be as well. To ensure data accuracy, it's important to regularly calibrate our measurement tools, conduct routine checks, and validate the data we collect. Reliability comes from consistency in our data collection methods, ensuring that the data is gathered the same way each time to allow for accurate comparisons and trend analysis.

## REGULAR REVIEW CYCLES

Setting up regular review cycles is a fundamental part of maintaining effective business processes. Establishing a schedule for these reviews ensures that we consistently evaluate and refine our operations, preventing issues from escalating and seizing opportunities for improvement. Reviews might be conducted weekly, monthly, or quarterly, depending on the nature of the process. Weekly reviews are useful for fast-moving processes that require constant attention, while monthly or quarterly reviews might be more appropriate for long-term projects or strategic initiatives.

Involving key stakeholders in these review cycles is crucial. Stakeholders can provide diverse perspectives and insights that might not be evident from the data alone. This includes managers, team members directly involved in the process, and sometimes even customers. Their input can help us understand how the process is working in practice and highlight any areas that need adjustment. During these reviews, we can discuss performance metrics, identify bottlenecks, and brainstorm solutions to any issues that arise.

## EMPLOYEE FEEDBACK

Employee feedback is another vital component of process evaluation. Gathering feedback from employees who are directly involved in the processes provides valuable insights into the day-to-day workings of our operations. Techniques for gathering this feedback can vary from surveys and suggestion boxes to regular team meetings and one-on-one discussions. The key is to make it easy for employees to share their thoughts and experiences.

Anonymous feedback is particularly important, as it encourages honesty and openness. Employees are more likely to share their true thoughts and concerns if they know their feedback cannot be traced back to them. This kind of feedback can reveal issues that might not be reported otherwise, such as inefficiencies or problems with team dynamics.

Once we have collected feedback, it's crucial to use it effectively. Analyzing the feedback helps us identify areas for improvement that might not be apparent from performance data alone. For instance, employees might highlight cumbersome procedures or suggest practical ways to streamline tasks. Implementing these suggestions improves the process and boosts morale, as employees feel heard and valued.

## Continuous Improvement

Continuous improvement is a core principle of effective process management. The concept revolves around the idea that no process is ever perfect and that there is always room for improvement. By fostering a culture of continuous improvement, we encourage everyone in the organization to constantly look for ways to enhance our operations. This mindset can significantly improve efficiency, quality, and employee satisfaction.

Strategies for fostering a culture of continuous improvement include encouraging open communication, providing training and resources for process improvement, and recognizing and rewarding employees who contribute valuable suggestions. It's about creating an environment where employees feel empowered to take initiative and where continuous improvement is part of the organizational DNA.

Examples of successful continuous improvement initiatives can be found in various industries. For instance, a manufacturing company might implement a new quality control process that reduces defects and waste. A retail business might refine its inventory management system to improve stock levels and reduce shortages. These initiatives often start small but can lead to significant long-term benefits.

## ADJUSTING BASED ON EVALUATION RESULTS

Adjusting based on evaluation results is a critical step in refining and improving our business processes. Once we have gathered and analyzed the evaluation data, the next step is to identify which adjustments are necessary. This involves looking closely at the data to pinpoint areas where performance is lacking or where there are inefficiencies. It's about understanding the root causes of any issues and determining the best ways to address them.

After identifying the necessary adjustments, the next task is to prioritize these improvements. Not all changes will have the same impact, and not all will be equally feasible. We need to weigh the potential benefits of each adjustment against the resources required to implement it. This means considering factors such as cost, time, and the availability of personnel. Improvements that offer the greatest impact with the least effort should be tackled first. However, sometimes more significant, resource-intensive changes might be necessary if they promise substantial long-term benefits.

Once we have prioritized the improvements, it's time to implement the changes. This step requires careful planning and clear communication with the team. Everyone needs to understand what changes are being made, why they are necessary, and how they will benefit the organization. Clear communication helps ensure the team is on board, and everyone knows their role in the new process.

Implementing changes effectively often involves training and support. Employees need to be equipped with the knowledge and tools to adapt to the new procedures. Providing training sessions, updated documentation, and a support system for any questions or issues that arise can facilitate a smooth transition. It's also important to monitor the implementation closely and be ready to address any unexpected challenges and make further adjustments if necessary.

For example, let's say our evaluation data shows that our customer service response times are longer than desired. By analyzing the data, we might discover that a particular step in the process is causing delays. We then prioritize improvements that could streamline this step, such as introducing a new software tool or redistributing tasks among team members. Once we decide on the changes, we communicate them clearly to the customer service team, explaining how the new procedures will work and why they are important. Training sessions help the team adapt to the new tool, and ongoing support ensures that any teething problems are quickly resolved.

## Overcoming Challenges in Monitoring and Evaluation

Overcoming challenges in monitoring and evaluating processes is crucial for maintaining the efficiency and effectiveness of our operations. One common challenge is the resistance to change. Employees might be comfortable with the current processes and wary of new evaluation methods. Another challenge is the availability and accuracy of data. Incomplete or inaccurate data can lead to incorrect conclusions and ineffective improvements. Additionally, the complexity of certain processes can make monitoring and evaluation difficult, as it might be hard to identify which metrics are most important.

To address these challenges, we must develop strategies fostering a culture of openness and continuous improvement. Communicating the benefits of monitoring and evaluation to the team can help overcome resistance. It's important to explain how these practices improve the business and make their jobs easier and more efficient. For data accuracy, we can implement standardized data collection methods and use reliable tools to ensure the information we gather is both complete and correct. Breaking complex processes down into smaller, manageable parts can make it easier to identify key metrics and evaluate performance effectively.

Flexibility and adaptability are essential in the evaluation process. No matter how well we plan, unexpected issues will arise. Being flexible means we can adjust our approach as needed, responding to new challenges and opportunities as they emerge. Adaptability allows us to refine our processes continuously, ensuring they remain relevant and effective in a changing business environment.

## TOOLS AND TECHNOLOGIES FOR MONITORING AND EVALUATION

When it comes to tools and technologies for monitoring and evaluation, there are many options available that can simplify and enhance our efforts. Software like project management tools, customer relationship management (CRM) systems, and business intelligence platforms can provide real-time data and analytics, making tracking performance and identifying trends easier. The benefits of using technology in process evaluation include increased accuracy, efficiency, and the ability to analyze large amounts of data quickly.

Selecting the right tools for our business needs involves assessing our specific requirements and choosing solutions that align with our goals. It's important to consider factors such as ease of use, scalability, and integration with existing systems. For instance, a CRM system that tracks customer interactions and feedback can be invaluable if we're looking to improve customer service. On the other hand, a manufacturing business might benefit more from an enterprise resource planning (ERP) system that monitors production processes and inventory levels.

## CONCLUSION

Monitoring and evaluating processes is essential for maintaining the efficiency and effectiveness of any business. By consistently assessing our operations, we can identify areas that need improvement, make informed decisions, and enhance overall performance. This continuous scrutiny helps us stay ahead of potential issues, ensuring that our processes remain robust and capable of meeting our goals.

Integrating these practices into our everyday operations is crucial. It shouldn't be an occasional activity but a fundamental part of how we operate. Regularly reviewing our processes and performance data allows us to make timely adjustments and keep everything running smoothly. By making monitoring and evaluation a routine aspect of our business, we can foster a culture of continuous improvement and accountability.

The long-term benefits of effective process management are substantial. Consistent monitoring and evaluation lead to better decision-making, increased efficiency, and higher-quality outcomes. When our processes are well-managed, we can respond more quickly to market changes, capitalize on new opportunities, and mitigate risks more effectively. This proactive approach not only enhances our current operations but also sets the stage for sustainable growth and success in the future.

In conclusion, the importance of monitoring and evaluating processes cannot be overstated. These practices help us maintain high standards, improve continuously, and achieve our business objectives. By embedding them into our daily routines, we ensure that our business remains agile, efficient, and competitive. The commitment to effective process management ultimately drives long-term success and positions us to thrive in an ever-changing business landscape.

# 6

# TECHNOLOGY AND
# AUTOMATION

Technology and automation have revolutionized the way businesses operate. They have streamlined processes, reduced costs, and increased productivity. This chapter will explore the impact of technology and automation on business processes, highlighting their benefits and the strategic steps necessary for successful implementation. We'll cover everything from understanding the role of technology in business to identifying areas ripe for automation and overcoming common challenges.

To begin, it's important to define what we mean by business technology. Business technology encompasses all the tools, systems, and applications that help manage and streamline operations. This includes everything from basic office software to complex enterprise resource planning (ERP) systems. The scope of business technology is broad, touching nearly every aspect of a company's operations, from communication and data management to customer service and financial transactions.

Historically, the evolution of business technology has been remarkable. In the early days, businesses relied on manual processes and simple tools. The advent of the personal com-puter and the internet transformed the landscape, introducing new ways to handle information and communicate. Over the years, we've seen a shift from basic digital tools to advanced automation and artificial intelligence. These advancements have changed how businesses operate and set new standards for efficiency and innovation.

Today, current trends in business technology focus heav-ily on automation, data analytics, and cloud computing. Automation tools, such as robotic process automation (RPA) and machine learning algorithms, are becoming more preva-lent, enabling businesses to automate repetitive tasks and make smarter decisions based on data analysis. Cloud computing has revolutionized data storage and accessibility, allowing businesses to operate more flexibly and collaboratively. These trends are shaping the future of business operations, pushing companies to adopt new technologies to stay competitive.

In summary, technology and automation profoundly impact business processes, driving efficiency and innovation. Understanding the evolution and current trends in business technology helps us appreciate its significance and prepares us for strategically implementing these tools in our opera-tions. In the following sections, we'll delve into the specifics of identifying areas for automation, selecting the right tools, and ensuring successful adoption and integration within your business.

## BENEFITS OF TECHNOLOGY AND AUTOMATION

The benefits of technology and automation in business are substantial, fundamentally transforming how we operate and compete in the market. One of the most significant advantages is the increase in efficiency and productivity. By automating routine tasks, we free up time for our employees to focus on more strategic, value-added activities. This shift boosts productivity and enhances job satisfaction, as employees can engage in more meaningful work rather than repetitive, mundane tasks.

Automation also plays a crucial role in reducing manual errors and improving accuracy. Human error is inevitable, especially in tasks that involve a lot of data entry or repetitive actions. However, automation tools can perform these tasks with a level of precision that humans cannot consistently achieve. This improved accuracy leads to better quality outputs and reduces the need for rework, saving both time and money.

Cost savings and resource optimization are other key benefits. While there is an upfront investment in technology, the long-term savings often outweigh these initial costs. Automated systems can handle tasks faster and more efficiently than human workers, saving significant labor costs. Additionally, optimizing resource use can reduce waste and improve overall operational efficiency. For instance, automated inventory management systems ensure that we only order what we need, reducing excess stock and minimizing storage costs.

Enhanced data management and analytics capabilities are also a major advantage of embracing technology and automation. Modern business technology allows us to collect and analyze vast amounts of data quickly and accurately. This capability provides valuable insights into our operations, customer behaviors, and market trends. With better data at our fingertips, we can make more informed decisions, tailor our strategies more effectively, and ultimately drive our business forward.

## IDENTIFYING AREAS FOR AUTOMATION

Identifying areas for automation in our business is essential for maximizing efficiency and productivity. The first step in this process is to establish criteria for selecting which processes are suitable for automation. Generally, tasks that are repetitive, time-consuming, and prone to human error are prime candidates. If a process involves a lot of manual data entry or requires the same steps to be performed consistently, it's likely a good fit for automation. We also look for tasks that can be easily defined and structured, as these are easier to automate effectively.

Some common business processes that benefit significantly from automation include inventory management, customer service, and finance. In inventory management, automation can help track stock levels in real time, generate orders automatically when supplies run low, and provide detailed analytics on inventory turnover. This reduces the risk of stockouts or overstocking and frees up staff to focus on more strategic activities, like sourcing new products or negotiating better deals with suppliers.

Customer service is another area where automation can make a big impact. Automated systems like chatbots can handle routine inquiries, process orders, and even troubleshoot common issues. This reduces the workload on human customer service agents, allowing them to focus on more complex and personalized customer interactions. The result is a more efficient service operation and improved customer satisfaction.

In finance, automation can streamline tasks such as invoicing, payroll processing, and expense reporting. Automated systems can ensure that invoices are sent out promptly, payments are processed on time, and financial reports are generated accurately. This enhances accuracy, reduces errors, and speeds up financial processes, providing better cash flow management and more timely financial insights.

One case study that highlights the successful implementation of automation is a mid-sized retail company that automated its inventory management system. Before automation, the company struggled with frequent stockouts and overstock situations, leading to lost sales and increased storage costs. By implementing an automated inventory management system, they were able to maintain optimal stock levels, reduce excess inventory, and improve order accuracy. This change boosted their efficiency and significantly improved their bottom line.

Another example is a financial services firm that automated its customer onboarding process. Previously, the onboarding process was manual and time-consuming, involving multiple steps and significant paperwork. By automating the process, they reduced the time it took to onboard new clients from several days to just a few hours. This increased client satisfaction and allowed the firm to scale its operations more effectively.

In summary, identifying areas for automation involves looking for repetitive, time-consuming tasks that can be clearly defined. Processes like inventory management, customer service, and finance often benefit greatly from automation. Successful case studies show that automation can significantly improve efficiency, accuracy, and overall business performance. By carefully selecting and implementing automation, we can drive our business forward and achieve greater success.

## TOOLS AND TECHNOLOGIES FOR AUTOMATION

When it comes to automating business processes, selecting the right tools and technologies is crucial. There are several popular automation tools and software options available that can help streamline operations and improve efficiency. Each of these tools offers unique features and benefits that can be tailored to meet the specific needs of a business.

Enterprise Resource Planning (ERP) systems are one of the most comprehensive automation tools available. They integrate various functions, such as inventory management, order processing, finance, and human resources, into a single system. The main advantage of an ERP system is that it provides a unified platform for all business operations, ensuring consistency and accuracy across different departments. With real-time data and analytics, ERP systems help make informed decisions and optimize resource allocation.

Customer Relationship Management (CRM) systems are another valuable automation tool. These systems focus on managing a company's interactions with current and potential customers. CRM systems can automate tasks like tracking customer inquiries, managing sales pipelines, and organizing customer data. The benefits include improved customer service, increased sales efficiency, and better customer insights, which can help tailor marketing strategies and improve customer retention.

Robotic Process Automation (RPA) is a technology that uses software robots to perform routine tasks that typically require human intervention. RPA can be used for a variety of functions, such as data entry, transaction processing, and compliance reporting. The key benefit of RPA is that it significantly reduces the time and effort required to perform repetitive tasks, allowing employees to focus on more strategic activities. RPA is highly scalable and can be adapted to handle increasing volumes of work without additional labor costs.

When selecting the right automation tools for our business, there are several considerations to keep in mind. First, we need to assess our specific needs and objectives. What are the key areas where automation can provide the most value? Understanding our current processes' pain points and bottlenecks will help us choose the most appropriate tools.

It's also important to consider the scalability and flexibility of the automation tools. As our business grows, we need systems that can scale with us and adapt to changing needs. Additionally, ease of integration with our existing systems and processes is a critical factor. The selected tools should seamlessly integrate with our current IT infrastructure to avoid disruptions and ensure a smooth transition.

Cost is another significant consideration. While automation tools can lead to long-term savings, the initial investment can be substantial. It's essential to evaluate the return on investment (ROI) and ensure that the benefits outweigh the costs. Additionally, we should look for tools that offer robust support and training to help our team get up to speed quickly and use the systems effectively.

For instance, when we decided to implement an ERP system, we chose one that could integrate with our existing accounting software and inventory management tools. This integration ensured we didn't have to overhaul our entire IT infrastructure, saving time and money. The ERP system provided real-time insights into our operations, allowing us to make better decisions and improve overall efficiency.

## IMPLEMENTING AUTOMATION

Implementing automation in a business involves careful planning and execution to ensure success. The first step in this process is to develop a clear plan. This plan should outline the specific processes we want to automate, the goals we hope to achieve, and the timeline for implementation. It's important to set realistic milestones and allocate resources effectively. A detailed plan serves as a roadmap, guiding us through each phase of the project and helping us stay on track.

Involving stakeholders early in the process is crucial for getting buy-in and ensuring a smooth implementation. Stakeholders can include employees using the new systems, managers overseeing these processes, and even customers who might be affected by the changes. By involving these key players from the beginning, we can address their concerns, gather valuable insights, and build support for the project. Clear communication about the benefits of automation and how it will improve their work can help alleviate any resistance to change.

Once we have a solid plan and stakeholder buy-in, the next step is to conduct pilot testing. Implementing automation on a small scale allows us to test the new systems in a controlled environment. This pilot phase helps us identify any issues and make necessary adjustments before a full rollout. By starting small, we can ensure that the new processes work as intended and minimize disruptions.

After a successful pilot test, we can proceed with gradual implementation. Rolling out the new systems in stages rather than all at once helps manage the transition more smoothly. This phased approach allows us to monitor progress, address any problems that arise, and make continuous improvements. Gradual implementation also gives employees time to adapt to the new processes, reducing the likelihood of resistance and errors.

Training employees is a critical component of implementing automation. Comprehensive training programs ensure that everyone understands how to use the new systems effectively. This training should be hands-on and practical, giving employees the opportunity to practice using the new tools in real-world scenarios. Providing ongoing support is equally important. Employees need to know that they can get help if they encounter issues or have questions. Setting up a help desk or a dedicated support team can provide the necessary assistance and ensure a smooth transition.

For example, when we automated our customer service processes, we started with a detailed plan outlining our goals and timeline. We then held meetings with our customer service team to explain the benefits of the new system and address any concerns. After gaining their support, we conducted a pilot test with a small group of agents. Based on their feedback, we made adjustments and gradually rolled out the system to the entire team. Comprehensive training sessions were held, and we set up a support hotline to help with any issues. This approach ensured a smooth transition and improved our customer service efficiency.

## Monitoring and Evaluating Automated Processes

Monitoring and evaluating automated processes is essential to ensure they deliver the intended benefits. To start, we need to establish key performance indicators (KPIs) for our automated systems. These KPIs serve as benchmarks, helping us measure the success of our automation efforts. They should be specific, measurable, and aligned with our overall business goals. For instance, if we've automated our inventory management, relevant KPIs might include inventory turnover rates, order accuracy, and stockout incidents. By tracking these metrics, we can gauge how well the automation is performing and whether it's meeting our objectives.

Once we have our KPIs in place, we need to implement techniques for monitoring performance and identifying any issues. Regularly reviewing these performance metrics is crucial. This can be done through automated reporting tools that provide real-time data and alerts for any anomalies. For example, if our KPIs show a sudden drop in order accuracy, this could indicate a problem with the automated system that needs immediate attention. Regular audits and checks help ensure that the system is functioning correctly and that any deviations are promptly addressed.

Another effective monitoring technique is gathering feedback from employees who interact with the automated processes. These individuals can offer valuable insights into any issues they encounter and suggest potential improvements. Encouraging a culture of open communication where employees feel comfortable sharing their experiences can lead to more effective monitoring and quicker resolution of problems.

Continuous improvement is vital for maintaining the effectiveness of our automated systems. Automation is not a set-it-and-forget-it solution; it requires regular updates and refinements. As our business evolves, so do our processes and the demands placed on our automated systems. Regularly reviewing and updating these systems ensures they continue to meet our needs and operate efficiently.

One approach to continuous improvement is to schedule periodic reviews of the automated processes. During these reviews, we can assess the performance data, gather user feedback, and identify areas for enhancement. This might involve updating the software to incorporate new features, adjusting the parameters of the automated tasks, or integrating additional tools to enhance functionality.

For example, after automating our customer support ticketing system, we established KPIs such as response time, resolution time, and customer satisfaction scores. By monitoring these metrics, we noticed an initial improvement in response times but identified a slight drop in customer satisfaction. Through employee feedback, we learned that while tickets were being resolved faster, the quality of responses needed attention. We addressed this by refining our automated responses and providing additional training to our support team. This continuous improvement approach helped us achieve both efficiency and high-quality customer service.

## Overcoming Challenges in Automation

Implementing automation in any business comes with its share of challenges and pitfalls. One of the most common issues is the disruption it can cause to existing workflows. Automation projects can sometimes lead to temporary inefficiencies as employees adjust to new systems. There's also the risk of technical problems that can arise during the transition, such as software bugs or compatibility issues with existing systems. These disruptions can cause frustration and slow down productivity, at least initially.

Another significant challenge is resistance to change. Employees who are used to doing things a certain way might be wary of new technology. They may fear that automation will make their jobs redundant or that they won't be able to adapt to new methods. This resistance can slow down the implementation process and undermine the effectiveness of the new systems.

Clear communication and involvement are key to addressing resistance to change. It's important to explain the reasons for the automation project, emphasizing how it will benefit both the business and the employees. Highlighting the ways in which automation can make their jobs easier and more efficient can help alleviate fears. Involving employees in the planning and implementation stages can also help. When employees feel they have a say in how the new systems are developed and used, they're more likely to buy into the changes.

Training and support are crucial in this process. Comprehensive training ensures employees understand how to use the new technology effectively. Ongoing support, such as help desks and troubleshooting resources, can help smooth the transition and address any issues that arise. By offering these resources, we can help employees feel more confident and capable as they adapt to the new systems.

Cybersecurity and data protection are other critical concerns in automation projects. Automated systems often handle large amounts of sensitive data, making them attractive targets for cyberattacks. Ensuring robust cybersecurity measures are in place is essential to protect this data. This includes implementing strong access controls, encrypting sensitive information, and regularly updating security protocols to guard against new threats.

Our business encountered several challenges when we decided to automate our financial reporting system. There was initial resistance from the finance team, who were comfortable with the existing manual processes. To address this, we held a series of meetings to explain the benefits of automation, such as reduced errors and faster reporting times. We also involved key team members in selecting and testing the new software, which helped them feel more invested in the project.

We worked with our IT department to implement strong security measures to ensure cybersecurity. We conducted thorough testing to identify and fix any vulnerabilities before the system went live. Regular audits and updates have helped us maintain a high level of data protection since then.

Overcoming challenges in automation requires careful planning, clear communication, and robust cybersecurity measures. By addressing resistance to change with transparency and support and ensuring that our automated systems are secure, we can implement automation projects successfully. These efforts improve efficiency and accuracy and help build a more resilient and adaptable business.

## THE FUTURE OF TECHNOLOGY AND AUTOMATION

The future of technology and automation holds immense potential for transforming business processes. Emerging technologies like artificial intelligence (AI), machine learning, blockchain, and the Internet of Things (IoT) are set to revolutionize the way we operate. These advancements promise to make our processes more efficient, accurate, and responsive to the market's changing needs.

Artificial intelligence and machine learning, in particular, are at the forefront of this transformation. AI can analyze vast amounts of data quickly, providing insights that were previously impossible to obtain. Machine learning algorithms can learn from this data, improving their performance over time and making predictions that help us make better business decisions. For example, AI can optimize supply chain operations by predicting demand patterns and adjusting inventory levels accordingly. This reduces waste and ensures that we can promptly meet customer demands.

Preparing our business for these technological advancements requires a proactive approach. It starts with staying informed about the latest developments in technology and understanding how they can be applied to our operations. This means regularly attending industry conferences, participating in webinars, and reading relevant publications. It's also essential to foster a culture of innovation within the company, encouraging employees to experiment with new tools and technologies and think creatively about how they can improve our processes.

Investing in training and development is another critical aspect of preparing for future technological advancements. As new technologies emerge, our employees need to have the skills and knowledge to use them effectively. Providing ongoing training and development opportunities ensures that our team stays ahead of the curve and can leverage new tools to their fullest potential.

The role of artificial intelligence and machine learning in automation cannot be overstated. These technologies can transform how we work, making our processes smarter and more efficient. For instance, AI-driven chatbots can handle routine customer service inquiries, freeing up human agents to deal with more complex issues. Machine learning algorithms can analyze customer data to identify trends and preferences, allowing us to personalize our marketing efforts and improve customer satisfaction.

To fully realize the benefits of AI and machine learning, we need to integrate them into our existing systems and processes. This involves working closely with technology providers to ensure that the new tools are compatible with our current infrastructure. It also means continuously monitoring and evaluating the performance of these technologies to ensure that they are delivering the expected benefits.

Looking ahead, the potential impact of emerging technologies on business processes is enormous. By staying informed, fostering a culture of innovation, investing in training, and integrating new tools into our operations, we can prepare our business for the future. Embracing these advancements will improve our efficiency and competitiveness and position us for long-term success in an ever-evolving market.

## Conclusion

Technology and automation play a crucial role in modern business. They drive efficiency, reduce errors, and help us stay competitive in an ever-changing market. Integrating advanced tools and systems into our operations allows us to streamline processes, save time, and make better decisions based on accurate data.

Embracing technological advancements is essential for long-term success. It's not just about keeping up with the latest trends but about strategically implementing solutions that align with our business goals. As new technologies emerge, we must be willing to adapt and innovate, using these tools to enhance our operations and deliver greater value to our customers.

The strategic implementation of technology and automation requires careful planning, clear communication, and ongoing evaluation. We must ensure that our employees are trained and supported, that our systems are secure, and that we continuously monitor performance to make necessary adjustments. By doing so, we can maximize the benefits of technology and create a more agile and resilient business.

The importance of technology and automation in today's business landscape cannot be overstated. These tools are key to achieving efficiency, accuracy, and competitiveness. By embracing and strategically implementing technological advancements, we can position our business for sustained growth and success in the years to come.

# 7

# BUILDING A CULTURE OF PROCESS EXCELLENCE

Building a culture of process excellence is crucial for any business that aims to achieve sustainable success. When we foster a culture that prioritizes process excellence, we set the stage for continuous improvement, innovation, and high performance across all areas of our operations. This culture is not just about following procedures; it's about creating an environment where every team member is committed to optimizing processes and delivering the highest quality work.

The importance of a process excellence culture cannot be overstated. It directly impacts efficiency, productivity, and quality, leading to better outcomes for both the business and its customers. When everyone in the organization is aligned with the principles of process excellence, we see fewer errors, reduced waste, and faster turnaround times. This, in turn, enhances customer satisfaction and drives business growth.

This chapter will explore what it means to build a culture of process excellence and why it's essential for our business. We'll start by defining process excellence and discussing its benefits, such as improved efficiency and increased employee engagement. We'll then delve into the critical role of leadership in setting the vision and goals for process excellence, leading by example, and providing the necessary resources and support for employees to succeed.

Next, we will discuss the importance of employee engagement and empowerment in achieving process excellence. We'll look at ways to involve employees in process improvement initiatives, build their skills and competencies, and recognize and reward their contributions. This section will highlight how empowering employees to take ownership of their work leads to higher motivation and better performance.

Creating a continuous improvement mindset is another key element we will cover. Encouraging innovation and creativity, establishing continuous improvement processes, and monitoring and measuring success are all crucial steps in maintaining momentum and sustaining efforts over the long term. We'll explore various frameworks and techniques, such as Lean, Six Sigma, and Kaizen, that can help embed a culture of continuous improvement within the organization.

We will also address the challenges that can arise when building a process excellence culture. Resistance to change is a common obstacle, and we'll discuss strategies for overcoming it and gaining buy-in from all levels of the organization. Maintaining momentum and ensuring sustained efforts will be another focus, with practical advice on keeping the focus on process excellence over time.

To provide real-world context, we'll include case studies and examples of organizations that have successfully built a culture of process excellence. These success stories will offer valuable insights and lessons that can be applied to our own efforts. Additionally, we'll examine some common pitfalls and challenges, providing guidance on how to avoid them and learn from others' experiences.

In conclusion, this chapter will recap the key points covered and reinforce the importance of fostering a culture of process excellence. By applying the concepts and strategies discussed, we can create an environment that supports continuous improvement and drives our business toward long-term success. Embracing process excellence is not just a one-time effort; it's an ongoing commitment to excellence in everything we do.

## Understanding Process Excellence

Understanding process excellence is fundamental to building a thriving and competitive business. Process excellence goes beyond simple process improvement. It's about creating and sustaining processes that consistently deliver high-quality results efficiently and effectively.

When we talk about process excellence, we're referring to the pursuit of optimizing every aspect of our business operations. This means ensuring that all processes are functioning well and continuously being refined to meet the highest standards. Unlike process improvement, which focuses on making specific enhancements, process excellence is an ongoing commitment to achieving the best possible performance across all operations.

The benefits of fostering a culture of process excellence are substantial. First, it leads to enhanced efficiency and productivity. When processes are streamlined and optimized, tasks are completed faster and with less effort. This efficiency frees up resources that can be redirected towards more strategic activities, driving overall productivity.

Improved quality and consistency are also key advantages. With well-defined and standardized processes, the quality of our products or services becomes more predictable and reliable. This consistency builds trust with our customers, as they know they can expect the same high standards every time they interact with our business. It reduces errors and rework, leading to cost savings and a stronger reputation.

Another significant benefit is increased employee satisfaction and engagement. When employees have clear processes to follow and understand how their work contributes to the business's overall success, they are more likely to feel valued and motivated. A culture of process excellence encourages employees to take ownership of their roles and strive for continuous improvement, fostering a more engaged and productive workforce.

Lastly, process excellence provides a competitive advantage and drives business growth. Companies that excel in their operations can respond more quickly to market changes, innovate more effectively, and deliver superior value to their customers. This agility and responsiveness help us stay ahead of competitors and seize new opportunities for growth.

For example, consider a company that has embraced process excellence in its manufacturing operations. By implementing lean manufacturing principles and continuously refining its production processes, the company can produce high-quality products faster and at a lower cost than its competitors. This efficiency allows the company to offer competitive pricing and invest in innovation, further strengthening its market position.

Understanding and pursuing process excellence is essential for any business looking to achieve long-term success. It's about more than just making improvements; it's about committing to a culture of continuous optimization and high standards. By focusing on process excellence, we can enhance efficiency, improve quality, boost employee engagement, and gain a competitive edge in the market. This commitment drives business growth and ensures that we remain resilient and adaptable in a constantly evolving landscape.

## LEADERSHIP'S ROLE IN FOSTERING PROCESS EXCELLENCE

Leadership plays a pivotal role in fostering process excellence within any organization. It all starts with setting a clear vision and goals. Without a well-defined vision, it's challenging to drive the commitment needed to achieve process excellence. A clear vision provides a sense of direction and purpose, guiding every team member towards a common objective. It's essential that this vision aligns with our overall business strategy. When process excellence is integrated into our strategic goals, it becomes a fundamental part of our business operations rather than a separate initiative.

As leaders, we must also lead by example. Demonstrating a personal commitment to process excellence sets the tone for the entire organization. When employees see that leadership is dedicated to optimizing processes and achieving high standards, they are more likely to follow suit. Our behavior as leaders significantly influences the organizational culture. If we are consistently focused on process improvement, attentive to details, and willing to invest the time and resources needed to enhance our operations, it fosters a culture where everyone values and strives for excellence.

Providing resources and support is another critical aspect of leadership in this context. Achieving process excellence requires the right tools, training, and technology investment. It's not enough to set high expectations; we must also ensure our employees have what they need to meet those expectations. This might involve upgrading software, investing in new equipment, or providing comprehensive training programs. Equipping our team with the necessary resources empowers them to perform at their best and drive continuous improvement.

For instance, if we aim to improve our customer service processes, we might need to invest in a new customer relationship management (CRM) system that streamlines interactions and tracks customer issues more effectively. Additionally, we would provide training for our customer service representatives on how to use the new system and handle common challenges. This combination of the right tools and proper training ensures that our team consistently delivers exceptional service.

Leaders must also create an environment where employees feel supported in their efforts to achieve process excellence. This means being available to address concerns, providing constructive feedback, and recognizing achievements. When employees know their efforts are appreciated and they have the backing of their leaders, they are more likely to take initiative and contribute to the continuous improvement of processes.

## EMPLOYEE ENGAGEMENT AND EMPOWERMENT

Employee engagement and empowerment are critical to achieving process excellence. When employees are actively involved in process improvement, they feel a stronger connection to their work and are more motivated to contribute to the organization's success. Encouraging their participation in process analysis and improvement initiatives is not just beneficial; it's essential.

To truly engage employees, we need to create an environment where their ideas and feedback are valued. One effective way to do this is by involving them directly in analyzing current processes. By inviting them to share their experiences and insights, we can uncover inefficiencies and identify opportunities for improvement that might not be evident from a managerial perspective. Techniques such as regular feedback sessions, suggestion boxes, and collaborative workshops can be instrumental in gathering this valuable input. When employees see that their feedback leads to tangible changes, their sense of ownership and commitment to the process grows.

Building skills and competencies is another vital aspect of fostering a culture of process excellence. Continuous training and development are necessary to equip our team with the latest knowledge and skills. Investing in comprehensive training programs ensures employees understand the principles of process excellence and can apply them in their daily tasks. Initiatives like workshops, online courses, and cross-training programs can help employees enhance their abilities and stay up-to-date with industry best practices. This ongoing development not only improves individual performance but also strengthens the overall capacity of the organization to implement and sustain process improvements.

Recognizing and rewarding excellence is crucial for maintaining high levels of motivation and engagement. When employees' efforts and achievements are acknowledged, it reinforces their commitment to maintaining high standards. Recognition can take many forms, from simple verbal praise and thank-you notes to more formal reward programs. For example, implementing an "Employee of the Month" program or offering bonuses for innovative process improvement ideas can significantly boost morale and encourage a culture of excellence. These programs should be designed to be fair and transparent, ensuring that all employees have the opportunity to be recognized for their contributions.

For instance, let's consider a scenario where a team member identifies a way to streamline the order fulfillment process, reducing delivery times by 20 percent. Acknowledging this achievement with a reward, such as a bonus or public recognition during a team meeting, motivates that individual and sets a positive example for others. It demonstrates that the organization values and rewards initiative and innovation.

Engaging and empowering employees is a cornerstone of process excellence. We create a motivated and capable workforce by involving them in process improvement, providing ongoing training and development, and recognizing their contributions. This approach enhances our operational efficiency and fosters a positive and dynamic organizational culture where employees feel valued and are driven to excel. The collective effort of an engaged and empowered team is what propels us toward sustained success and continuous improvement.

## CREATING A CONTINUOUS IMPROVEMENT MINDSET

Creating a continuous improvement mindset is essential for sustaining long-term success in any business. Encouraging innovation and creativity is the first step in this journey. To foster an environment where new ideas are welcomed and explored, we need to create a culture that values open communication and experimentation. This means not only being open to new ideas but actively seeking them out. We can do this by organizing brainstorming sessions, encouraging cross-departmental collaboration, and celebrating innovative thinking. When employees feel that their ideas are valued, they are more likely to contribute creative solutions to everyday challenges.

To stimulate innovative thinking, we can use techniques like brainstorming workshops, innovation contests, and think tanks. These initiatives provide structured opportunities for employees to share their ideas and collaborate on potential solutions. For example, we could hold a monthly innovation meeting where team members present their ideas for process improvements, no matter how small. This generates a wealth of ideas and fosters a sense of ownership and pride in the team's collective creativity.

Establishing continuous improvement processes involves implementing structured frameworks such as Lean, Six Sigma, and Kaizen. These methodologies provide systematic approaches to identifying inefficiencies, reducing waste, and enhancing quality. Lean focuses on maximizing value by eliminating waste, Six Sigma aims to reduce variability and defects, and Kaizen emphasizes small, incremental changes for continuous improvement. By adopting these frameworks, we can create a disciplined approach to process excellence that is sustainable over the long term.

Regular review cycles and feedback loops are crucial components of these frameworks. Regular review cycles ensure we continuously evaluate our processes and make necessary adjustments. Feedback loops allow us to gather insights from employees and stakeholders, ensuring that our improvements are aligned with their needs and expectations. For instance, we could implement quarterly process review meetings where we assess the effectiveness of recent changes and identify new areas for improvement. These meetings provide a structured forum for discussing progress and planning next steps.

Monitoring and measuring success is vital to understanding the impact of our continuous improvement efforts. Tracking progress and measuring outcomes allow us to see what is working and what needs further refinement. Key performance indicators (KPIs) for process excellence include cycle time, error rates, customer satisfaction, and employee engagement. These indicators provide quantifiable data that help us assess the effectiveness of our improvements and make informed decisions about where to focus our efforts next.

For example, if we implement a new process to reduce order fulfillment times, we would track metrics such as the average time to fulfill an order, the number of orders processed per day, and customer feedback on delivery times. By regularly reviewing these KPIs, we can determine whether the new process is achieving its intended goals and identify any adjustments needed to enhance its effectiveness.

Creating a continuous improvement mindset involves encouraging innovation and creativity, establishing structured improvement processes, and diligently monitoring and measuring success. We can drive sustained improvement and excellence in our operations by fostering an environment that values new ideas, implementing proven methodologies, and tracking our progress. This approach enhances our efficiency and quality and builds a culture of continuous growth and innovation, positioning our business for long-term success.

## OVERCOMING CHALLENGES TO BUILDING A PROCESS EXCELLENCE CULTURE

Building a culture of process excellence is not without its challenges. One of the biggest hurdles we often face is resistance to change. Change can be unsettling, and it's natural for people to cling to familiar routines and practices. Understanding the common sources of resistance is the first step in addressing this challenge. Often, resistance stems from a fear of the unknown, concerns about job security, or a lack of understanding of the benefits that the changes will bring.

We need to employ strategies to build buy-in and support to overcome resistance. This starts with clear and transparent communication. People need to understand why changes are necessary and how they will positively impact both the organization and their roles. We should take the time to explain the benefits of process excellence and share success stories that highlight tangible improvements. Providing opportunities for employees to ask questions and voice their concerns is also crucial. We can alleviate fears and build trust by actively listening and addressing their worries.

Involving employees in the change process is another effective way to reduce resistance. When people feel they have a stake in the changes and their input is valued, they are more likely to support the initiatives. This can be done by forming cross-functional teams to work on process improvement projects or seeking employee feedback at all levels. Making them part of the solution fosters a sense of ownership and commitment.

Maintaining momentum and sustaining efforts toward process excellence is another challenge. It's easy to start strong but harder to keep the focus over the long term. One technique for keeping the momentum going is to set short-term goals and celebrate milestones. Recognizing and rewarding achievements, no matter how small, keeps the team motivated and reinforces the importance of continuous improvement.

Continuous communication and reinforcement play a vital role in sustaining efforts. Regular updates on progress, successes, and next steps keep everyone informed and engaged. This can be done through team meetings, newsletters, or internal bulletins. Sharing data and metrics that show the impact of process improvements helps to maintain a focus on results and accountability.

For example, if we've implemented a new inventory management system that reduces stockouts and overstock, we should regularly share data showing the reduction in inventory costs and improved order fulfillment rates. Highlighting these successes demonstrates the value of the changes and encourages a culture of data-driven decision-making.

Moreover, leaders must consistently demonstrate their commitment to process excellence. When leaders model the behaviors and attitudes they want to see in others, it sets a powerful example. This includes being open to feedback, continuously seeking ways to improve, and recognizing the efforts of the team. Leadership's visible commitment helps embed process excellence into the organizational culture, making it a daily routine rather than a one-off initiative.

Overcoming challenges to building a culture of process excellence requires addressing resistance to change and maintaining momentum over the long term. Understanding the sources of resistance and actively building buy-in can ease the transition and foster a supportive environment. Sustaining efforts involves continuous communication, celebrating successes, and strong leadership commitment. With these strategies, we can create a resilient and dynamic culture that embraces process excellence as a core value, driving sustained success and growth.

## CONCLUSION

As we conclude this chapter, it's clear that building a culture of process excellence is crucial for any business aiming for long-term success. We've discussed how such a culture enhances efficiency, quality, and employee engagement while providing a competitive edge. We set a strong foundation for sustainable growth and innovation by prioritizing process excellence.

We explored several strategies and techniques essential for fostering this culture. Leadership plays a pivotal role in setting the vision and goals, leading by example, and providing the necessary resources and support. Engaging and empowering employees through involvement in process improvement, continuous training, and recognition programs is equally important. Creating a mindset of continuous improvement by encouraging innovation, establishing structured improvement processes, and diligently monitoring progress ensures that we stay on the path to excellence.

Addressing resistance to change and maintaining momentum are challenges we must tackle head-on. Understanding common sources of resistance and implementing strategies to build buy-in can ease transitions and foster a supportive environment. Sustaining efforts requires continuous communication, celebrating successes, and strong leadership commitment.

I encourage you to apply these concepts within your organization. Building a culture of process excellence isn't a one-time effort but an ongoing commitment. Start by setting clear goals, involving your team in the process, and providing the necessary tools and support. Celebrate the small wins and learn from the setbacks. Doing so will create a dynamic and resilient organization capable of adapting to changes and continuously improving.

In the long run, a culture of process excellence will yield significant benefits. It will drive efficiency and productivity, enhance customer satisfaction, and boost employee morale. More importantly, it will position your business to thrive in an ever-evolving market landscape. Embrace the journey of continuous improvement, and you will see your organization flourish and achieve new heights of success.

# CONCLUSION

As we reach the end of this book, it's important to reflect on the key concepts we've covered and understand how they tie together to create a stronger, more efficient business.

First, we explored the importance of internal processes. These are the backbone of any organization, guiding daily operations and ensuring that tasks are completed consistently and efficiently. Well-defined internal processes help maintain order and drive productivity, enabling us to effectively meet our business goals.

Next, we delved into process mapping and identifying bottlenecks. Process mapping allows us to visualize each step of our operations, making it easier to spot inefficiencies and areas for improvement. Identifying bottlenecks can address the specific points in our processes that slow us down or cause disruptions. This step is crucial for streamlining our workflows and boosting overall efficiency.

We then discussed the importance of designing effective processes. This involves creating clear, structured procedures that everyone in the organization can follow. Effective processes reduce errors, improve quality, and ensure that tasks are completed on time. They provide a solid foundation for our operations and support consistent, high-quality output.

Implementing new procedures and fostering continuous improvement was another key topic. Change is a constant in the business world, and adapting and refining our processes is essential for staying competitive. By regularly reviewing and updating our procedures, we can respond to new challenges and opportunities, ensuring that our operations remain relevant and effective.

Finally, we looked at the role of technology and automation in modern business. Technology advances have revolutionized how we operate, offering tools that enhance efficiency, reduce manual errors, and provide valuable data insights. Automation allows us to handle repetitive tasks quickly and accurately, freeing up our time for more strategic activities.

Understanding and optimizing our internal processes, designing effective procedures, and leveraging technology and automation are all critical components of successful business management. Integrating these concepts into our daily operations can create a more efficient, productive, and adaptable organization. The journey of continuous improvement is ongoing, but with these tools and strategies, we are well-equipped to navigate the challenges and seize the opportunities that come our way.

## The Importance of Technology and Automation in Modern Business

Technology and automation have become indispensable in modern business, transforming how we operate and compete. Their impact is felt across all areas of our operations, driving us to new levels of efficiency and productivity.

One of the most significant benefits is the enhancement of efficiency and productivity. Automation streamlines routine tasks, allowing us to complete them faster and with less effort. This means that our employees can focus on more strategic activities that add value to the business rather than getting bogged down by repetitive work. For example, automated scheduling systems can manage appointments and meetings, freeing up administrative staff to handle more complex tasks.

Moreover, automation reduces manual errors and improves accuracy. Human error is a natural part of any manual process, but technology can minimize these mistakes. Automated systems follow precise instructions without deviation, ensuring that tasks are completed correctly every time. This leads to higher quality outputs and fewer errors that need to be corrected later, saving both time and resources.

Cost savings and resource optimization are also key advantages. While there may be an initial investment in technology, the long-term savings are substantial. Automation reduces the need for manual labor, cutting down on labor costs. It also optimizes the use of resources by ensuring that they are allocated efficiently and used effectively. For instance, inventory management systems can track stock levels in real time, preventing overordering and reducing storage costs.

Enhanced data management and analytics capabilities are another major benefit. Modern technology allows us to collect and analyze vast amounts of data quickly and accurately. This data provides valuable insights into our operations, helping us make informed decisions and identify areas for improvement. For example, customer relationship management (CRM) systems can analyze customer interactions and feedback, providing insights into customer preferences and behaviors. This information can be used to tailor marketing strategies and improve customer satisfaction.

The importance of technology and automation in modern business cannot be overstated. They enhance efficiency and productivity, reduce manual errors, save costs, and improve data management. By embracing these tools, we can operate more effectively, make better decisions, and stay competitive in an ever-evolving market. The benefits are clear, and the potential for future growth and success is immense.

Embracing technological advancements is essential for staying competitive and driving growth in today's fast-paced business environment. Adapting to new tools and technologies can seem daunting, but it's necessary to ensure our business remains efficient and relevant. We need to be open to change and willing to invest in new systems that can streamline our operations and enhance our capabilities.

It's important to encourage our team to explore new ideas and approaches to foster a culture of innovation and continuous learning. This means creating an environment where experimentation is welcomed and where employees feel comfortable suggesting improvements. By promoting a mindset of innovation, we can continually find better ways to do things and stay ahead of the competition.

Investing in employee training and development is crucial when introducing new technologies. Our team needs to be equipped with the skills and knowledge to use these tools effectively. Providing comprehensive training programs and ongoing development opportunities ensures that our employees can adapt to new systems and maximize their potential. This investment improves individual performance and strengthens our overall business capabilities.

Staying ahead of industry trends and advancements is another key aspect of embracing technological change. This involves keeping a close eye on developments in our field and being proactive in adopting new technologies that can give us a competitive edge. By staying informed and agile, we can quickly implement and leverage the latest innovations to our advantage.

When it comes to the strategic implementation of technology and automation, effective planning and execution are critical. The first step is to develop a clear plan that outlines our goals, identifies the necessary resources, and sets realistic timelines. This plan serves as a roadmap, guiding us through each phase of the implementation process.

Involving stakeholders and gaining their buy-in is essential for a successful implementation. Stakeholders, including employees, managers, and customers, need to understand the benefits of the new technology and how it will impact them. By involving them in planning and addressing their concerns, we can build support and ensure a smoother transition.

Pilot testing and gradual implementation are effective strategies for managing change. By starting with a small-scale test, we can identify any issues and make adjustments before rolling out the technology across the entire organization. This approach minimizes disruptions and allows us to refine the system based on real-world feedback.

Training and ongoing support for employees are vital to successfully adopting new technologies. Comprehensive training programs help employees understand how to use the new tools effectively, while ongoing support provides assistance as they adapt. This support can include help desks, user manuals, and regular check-ins to address any challenges that arise.

Embracing technological advancements requires a proactive and strategic approach. By adapting to new tools, fostering a culture of innovation, investing in training, and staying ahead of industry trends, we can position our business for long-term success. With careful planning, stakeholder involvement, pilot testing, and continuous support, we can effectively implement new technologies and reap the benefits of increased efficiency, productivity, and competitiveness.

## Overcoming Challenges

Overcoming challenges in business is never easy, but it is essential for growth and success. One of the biggest hurdles we often face is resistance to change. Employees may feel comfortable with the current way of doing things and hesitant about adopting new methods or technologies. Clear communication is key to addressing this. We need to explain the reasons behind the changes, the benefits they bring, and how they will make everyone's jobs easier. Involving employees in the process and seeking their input can also help ease their concerns and build support for the changes.

Ensuring cybersecurity and data protection is another critical challenge, especially as we adopt more technology and automation. Protecting our data from breaches and ensuring our systems are secure is paramount. This means investing in robust security measures like firewalls, encryption, and regular security audits. We must also train our employees on best practices for data security, making them aware of potential threats and how to avoid them.

Monitoring and evaluating automated processes is essential to ensure they are functioning as intended. By regularly reviewing performance data and gathering feedback from users, we can identify any issues and make necessary adjustments. This ongoing evaluation helps us maintain the effectiveness of our systems and ensures they continue to meet our needs.

Continuous improvement and updates to our systems are vital for staying ahead of the competition. Technology is always evolving, and what works today might not be as effective tomorrow. By committing to regular updates and improvements, we can ensure our processes remain efficient and effective. This involves staying informed about new advancements, seeking feedback from employees, and being willing to make changes when needed.

## LONG-TERM BENEFITS OF EFFECTIVE PROCESS MANAGEMENT

Effective process management brings long-term benefits that are essential for any successful business. One of the most significant advantages is improved operational efficiency. When we streamline our processes, we eliminate unnecessary steps, reduce waste, and ensure that tasks are completed accurately and promptly. This efficiency allows us to make the best use of our resources, which translates into cost savings and higher productivity. For example, by automating routine tasks, we can free up our employees to focus on more strategic activities that drive the business forward.

Enhanced customer satisfaction is another critical benefit. When our internal processes are well-managed, we can deliver products and services more reliably and consistently. Customers notice when their orders are processed quickly, inquiries are handled efficiently, and issues are resolved promptly. Satisfied customers are more likely to return and recommend our business to others, fostering loyalty and boosting our reputation. This level of service is only possible when our processes are designed to meet and exceed customer expectations.

Increased competitiveness in the market is also a direct result of effective process management. We can stay ahead of our competitors by continually refining and improving our processes. This proactive approach allows us to respond swiftly to market changes, innovate more effectively, and offer better value to our customers. When we operate efficiently, we can lower our costs and pass those savings on to our customers, making our offerings more attractive compared to those of our competitors.

Sustainable business growth and success are the ultimate goals of effective process management. Our business can scale more easily when we have solid processes in place. We can take on more clients, handle larger volumes of work, and expand into new markets without the chaos that often accompanies rapid growth. Effective processes provide a stable foundation that supports long-term growth. They help us maintain high standards of quality and service even as we expand, ensuring that we don't lose sight of what made us successful in the first place.

## FINAL THOUGHTS

As we wrap up this discussion on effective process management, it's clear that its role in business success is critical. Streamlined processes are the backbone of any efficient operation. They ensure that tasks are completed consistently and accurately, reducing errors and boosting productivity. Without well-defined processes, a business can quickly descend into chaos, with missed deadlines, poor quality, and dissatisfied customers.

However, process management is not a one-time task. It's an ongoing journey of improvement and adaptation. The business environment is constantly changing, and we must be ready to evolve with it. This means regularly reviewing and refining our processes to ensure they remain effective and aligned with our goals. It's about being proactive, not reactive, and always looking for ways to do things better.

I encourage you to integrate these practices into your daily operations. Make process management a part of your routine. Train your team to understand the importance of following established procedures and to look for opportunities to improve them. Encourage feedback and be open to suggestions. When everyone in the organization is committed to process improvement, the results can be transformative.

Looking to the future, we must embrace innovation and leverage technology for continuous growth. The rapid advancement of technology presents incredible opportunities to enhance our processes and drive efficiency. We can implement solutions that give us a competitive edge by staying informed about new tools and trends. Automation, artificial intelligence, and data analytics are just a few areas where we can make significant strides.

In conclusion, effective process management is the foundation of a successful business. It requires a commitment to continuous improvement and a willingness to adapt to changing circumstances. By integrating these practices into our daily operations and embracing technological innovation, we can position ourselves for sustained growth and success. Let's commit to this journey together, striving for excellence in everything we do and always looking for ways to improve. The future is bright for those who are willing to innovate and evolve.

# Work Less and Make More Money Than Ever Before

Take your business to the next level
with a fresh perspective.

Jason Miller's insights show you exactly how to break
through plateaus and achieve big profits.

Go beyond your expectations and
see what's possible for your business.

**jetlaunch.link/SABdiscover**

# About the Author

Jason Miller is an accomplished business leader with over thirty years of experience, renowned for his expertise in hyper company growth, scaling, and strategic and operational implementation. He founded the Strategic Advisor Board (SAB) in 2017 and served as its Senior Global Council Member, overseeing its global operations and team capabilities. In addition to his primary role at SAB, Jason holds multiple chair positions across various companies and nonprofits. He has built more than twenty-four companies from scratch since 2001 and is dedicated to crafting sustainable business models emphasizing leadership responsibility, strategy, and accountability.

Known for his no-excuses approach and nicknamed "The Bull," Jason has advised thousands of global leaders. He has been recognized as a foremost expert in consulting for creating scalable business models, particularly for small and mid-market companies. His focus extends to fostering a positive company culture, enhancing staff retention, and deepening customer loyalty, believing that a clear vision and purpose are essential for impactful business. As a veteran, Jason is committed to serving veteran-owned companies and provides pro bono services to veteran organizations as part of a five-year plan.

Jason holds an MBA from Trident University and credits the "school of hard knocks" for his doctorate in practical experience. He is affiliated with numerous prestigious organizations that impact business globally, such as the American Club Association, Leigh Steinberg Academy, Forbes Council, and Entrepreneur Magazine Leadership Council. A lifetime member of the American Legion, Disabled American Veterans, and Veterans of Foreign Wars, Jason lives in Boulder, Colorado, with his family. He focuses on professional development and business strategy to serve his clients better.